Razia
Queen of India

Razia
Queen of India

Rafiq Zakaria

Foreword by
P. B. Gajendragadkar

Preface by
K. A. Nilakanta Sastri

Illustrations by
Shiavax Chavda

UNIVERSITY PRESS

OXFORD

UNIVERSITY PRESS

Great Clarendon Street, Oxford OX2 6DP

Oxford University Press is a department of the University of Oxford.
It furthers the University's objective of excellence in research, scholarship,
and education by publishing worldwide in

Oxford New York

Athens Auckland Bangkok Bogotá Buenos Aires Calcutta
Cape Town Chennai Dar es Salaam Delhi Florence Hong Kong Istanbul
Karachi Kuala Lumpur Madrid Melbourne Mexico City Mumbai
Nairobi Paris São Paulo Singapore Taipei Tokyo Toronto Warsaw

with associated companies in Berlin Ibadan

Oxford is a registered trade mark of Oxford University Press
in the UK and in certain other countries

ISBN 0 19 579360 9

This edition published 1999 by Oxford University Press, Pakistan.
Reprinted by permission Popular Prakashan Private Limited, 35-C Pandit
M. M. M. Marg, Popular Press Building, Tardeo, Mumbai 400 034, India.

Printed in Pakistan at
New Sketch Graphics, Karachi.
Published by
Ameena Saiyid, Oxford University Press
5-Bangalore Town, Sharae Faisal
PO Box 13033, Karachi-75350, Pakistan.

To
Fatma
whose dedication
to human understanding
set me on a deeper quest
of Razia

CONTENTS

LIST OF ILLUSTRATIONS

Illustrations by Shiavax Chavda

FOREWORD

WHEN the serial publication of *Razia: Queen of India* came to an end, the Editor, Mr. A. S. Raman, announced in the columns of the *Illustrated Weekly of India* that he had received many letters from readers suggesting the prolongation of the story. The account of the life and reign of Queen Razia is in a sense history and fiction combined. From the letters received by Mr. Raman from the readers of the story, it is a safe inference that those who wanted to know about the story of Razia as a matter of history were satisfied and those who were interested in reading the artistic presentation of her reign were also happy. Both categories of readers thus appear to have been satisfied and that affords a true measure of the quality and success of the serialisation.

Dr. Rafiq Zakaria is not new to literature. A lawyer by training, a politician by profession, a young, progressive, forward-looking intellectual, irrevocably committed to democracy and dedicated to the cause of secularism, Dr. Zakaria takes a keen interest in the pursuit of literature. Unlike the ordinary pattern of educated Indians in several liberal professions, Dr. Zakaria does not concentrate exclusively on his work as a politician. If a lawyer is confined to law, a doctor to medicine, and an engineer to his own craft, they may lead a successful life in a professional sense; but considered as integrated human life, their career appears to be incomplete and suffers from an element of insufficiency or inadequacy. The true test of a full intellectual life is the pursuit of some other vocation in addition to one's own calling. Dr. Zakaria belongs to this category of Indian intellectuals. The pursuit of knowledge, the study of history and the urge to create literature, naturally, give to Dr. Zakaria's life a meaning, purpose and significance.

In fact, in his early life Dr. Zakaria was interested in journalism. He had his training on *The Observer*, London, and was for some time attached to SHAEF as a war correspondent. Later he contributed articles to several leading Indian newspapers and they attracted attention from the discerning public because of his style, his thoughts and the attractive man-

ner in which he presented his views. Even after he entered
active public life, Dr. Zakaria has not forgotten his love for
literature.

Before undertaking the task of writing the story of Razia,
Dr. Zakaria worked on the theme for more than seven years.
The recorded material about the life and career of Razia is
very scanty; but the subject fascinated Dr. Zakaria and he made
an earnest endeavour to study all the available material that
would give him a comprehensive picture of Razia, her character,
her views, her philosophy and her achievements. *The
Cambridge History of India* and the Bharatiya Vidya Bhavan's
monumental history were, surprisingly, of not much assistance
to him. Discussion of Razia and her career occupied a very
minor place in the accounts contained in these two histories.
Dr. Zakaria turned, therefore, to *Tabakat-i-Nasiri*, written by the
chronicler of the times, *Minhajus Seraj*. He also consulted the
original sources dealing with Razia's period. Some of them were
in the form of manuscripts such as Fakhr-i-Mudabbir's *Adab-ul-
Harb* in the British Museum and *Adab-ul Muluk* in the India
Office Library and his monumental work: *Bahrul Ansab*. A
portion of the last-named work has been edited by Sir Denison
Ross. Dr. Zakaria also scanned through Sadruddin Hasan
Nizami's *Tajul Ma'asir*, Yahya Sirhindi's *Tarikh-i-Mubarakshahi*
and Salim's *Riyazus Salatin*. Having thus exhaustively and
patiently consulted all the relevant material available on the
subject of Razia's life and career, Dr. Zakaria set about the task
of presenting the story in his work: *Razia: Queen of India*.
It is thus plain that the author has evolved the present story of
Razia from scanty material which had to be discovered in some
cases from almost inaccessible sources. His intensive research
spread over many years was obviously inspired by a sense of
fascination which Dr. Zakaria felt for the career of Razia. This
fascination has found expression in the evocative style which he
has adopted in narrating the story of the Queen.

Razia who is the only woman crowned in Delhi reigned for a
brief span of a little less than four years. Her father, Sultan
Shamsuddin Iltutmish, died on April 29, 1236. Thereafter, contrary to the direction expressed by the departed Sultan in his will,
the nobles of the kingdom put the Sultan's son Ruknuddin on
the throne with the assistance of his mother, Shah Turkan. The
young emperor turned out to be profligate as was apprehended

by his father and his rule came to an inglorious end on November 9, 1236; on this day, both he and his mother were ordered to be hanged. Razia thus ascended the throne amidst the applause and acclaim of the populace, though with the somewhat reluctant approval of the nobles. She was killed on the battle-field along with her husband, Altunia, on October 13, 1240. Dr. Zakaria has narrated the story beginning with the death of Razia's father and ending with her death on the battle-field; and though the period covered is a short span of about four years, yet Dr. Zakaria's pen has made the story lively and even thrilling.

In his epilogue, Dr. Zakaria has clearly indicated the purpose he had in mind in writing the story and the motive which inspired him. Is the story depicted by Dr. Zakaria history or is it fiction? The author faces this problem squarely and courageously and gives a clear answer to it. There is no ambivalence about the author's approach, no hesitation in his attitude and no ambiguity in his views in this matter. Some historians no doubt insist that the writing of history properly so called must be content to present facts as they occur; "let the facts speak for themselves" they say. Dr. Zakaria does not subscribe to this theory. He feels that facts are not necessarily capable of speaking for themselves and so he does not believe in allowing the facts to speak for themselves. In history, according to Dr. Zakaria, facts must be properly presented and the presentation of the facts is an art which would inevitably influence and lend colour to, the account. It is true that in presenting the facts, the first duty of an author is to ascertain the facts, but in this connection Dr. Zakaria has himself referred to the dictum of Professor Arnold Toynbee as to the three-fold method which the historian must adopt: First he must ascertain the facts and record them; secondly he must elucidate them through a comparative study of the facts ascertained; and thirdly he must be gifted with the power of the artistic recreation of the facts in the form of fiction. I do not know whether purists would agree but Dr. Zakaria has chosen to discard the purely orthodox view in this matter.

The historian's picture of the past, says Dr. Zakaria, in many details may be more imaginative and imaginary; he may develop resemblance to the novelist, but there is no need to be apologetic about it. Dr. Zakaria relies on Professor Collingwood, who has observed: "As works of imagination, the historian's work and the novelist's do not differ. Where they do differ is that the historian's picture is meant to be true. The novelist has a single task only: to construct a coherent picture, one that makes sense. The historian has a double task: he has both to do this, and to construct a picture of things as they really were and of events as they really happened."

In his epilogue, Dr. Zakaria makes no secret of the fact that in his presentation of Razia he had been guided by the preconceptions, the assumptions and the generalisations of his own experience, which are a part of his intellectual approach. These factors, he concedes, are evident not only in his treatment of Razia but the lesser figures, who played their roles in the drama of her life. "I have used the material," says the author, " in the same manner as a potter uses the clay, or the mason the stone, fashioning it to my heart's desire." It is thus clear that in writing the story of Razia he has been influenced by his " own idea as to what ought to be ".

In writing the present book Dr. Zakaria wanted to portray the life and career of a progressive Queen who ruled in Delhi in the middle ages; and he undertook this task because he found that in so doing he would be able to give artistic expression to what he regards as the basic concepts of good political, social and economic life. It would therefore be idle to apply to the story merely the purists' test of history writing; just as it would be unreasonable to treat it merely as fiction. It purports to be a harmonious combination of history and fiction. Dr. Zakaria has done his best to remain faithful to facts while in the development of the story and the depiction of events he has strenuously tried to be loyal to his own philosophy of life.

Considered merely as a story or fiction, apart from its historical basis and the concepts which have inspired the author in presenting it, it may be reasonably stated that the style adopted by the author is clear, lucid and expressive. The stream of the narrative is generally smooth. It, however, becomes vigorous and dynamic, corresponding with the nature of the situation or the particular incident described. The headings of the chapters are eloquent and the development of the story shows an artistic workmanship of a high order.

The description of the character of Razia has naturally received the attention of the author in a very large measure.

Razia was an enlightened ruler, progressive in outlook, dynamic in action; and she wanted to introduce several reforms during her regime. She was against the conservative and orthodox spirit of her time, and she knew that her Amirs and Maliks were never able to adjust themselves completely to the fact that a woman was ruling over them. They admired her courage and her wisdom, they appreciated her spirit of service, they applauded her ability as a warrior and a politician; nevertheless they always distrusted her progressive outlook and their loyalty to her was given invariably with a measure of reluctance.

Even so, the author recognises that Razia was a woman and he has described her strength and her foibles as a woman in very delicate words. Altunia loved Razia deeply, but he found it difficult to penetrate the armour of her aloofness. He made valiant efforts to make her lose herself in the ecstasies of an intimate, human relationship. He made, no doubt, some progress; but never quite succeeded. " There was," says the author, " something inexplicable about her, which held her back. Whether it was a psychological block or complete absorption in the affairs of the empire, or whether it was her orthodox upbringing or the fear of consequences, whatever it be, Razia would not let her emotions have the better of her. No sooner was she drawn into the whirlpool of romance than she managed to get out of it. It seemed as if she had some peculiar dread of the outcome."

In course of time, her relations with Jamaluddin Yaqut became very friendly. Yaqut was an Abyssynian slave; he was a brave soldier, a wise counsellor and dedicated friend of Razia. Their relationship naturally gave rise to whispers all round. Dr. Zakaria is righteously indignant at the uncharitable criticism made by historians in regard to her relationship with Yaqut. In his epilogue he has referred to this aspect of Razia's life in some detail and has observed that " no one, with any modicum of historical understanding would agree with the denunciation of the Queen and Yaqut indulged in by Farishta and others ". He adds that a good historian should avoid moral condemnation, especially where evidence is so slim and sketchy, and where many other factors lead overwhelmingly to a different conclusion. This criticism merely illustrates the significance of the ancient Sanskrit saying that in the case of the virtue of women as in the case

of the merit or quality of literature, men are apt to be cynical
and cruel.*

Prof. E. H. Carr in his G. M. Trevelyan lectures delivered in
the University of Cambridge puts the whole question in its true
perspective:

" The relation of history to morality is more complicated,
and discussions of it in the past have suffered from several
ambiguities. It is scarcely necessary today to argue that the
historian is not required to pass moral judgements on the
private life of the characters in his story. The standpoints
of the historian and of the moralist are not identical. Henry
VIII may have been a bad husband and a good king. But
the historian is interested in him in the former capacity only
in so far as it affected historical events. If his moral de-
linquencies had had as little apparent effect on public affairs
as those of Henry II, the historian would not need to bother
about them. This goes for virtues as well as vices. Pasteur
and Einstein were, one is told, men of exemplary, even saintly,
private lives. But, suppose they had been unfaithful hus-
bands, cruel fathers, and unscrupulous colleagues, would their
historical achievements have been any the less? And it is
these which preoccupy the historian. Stalin is said to have
behaved cruelly and callously to his second wife; but, as a
historian of Soviet affairs, I do not feel myself much concerned.
This does not mean that private morality is not important,
or that the history of morals is not a legitimate part of history.
But the historian does not turn aside to pronounce moral
judgements on the private lives of individuals who appear in
his pages. He has other things to do."

Dr. Zakaria has described Razia's feelings for Yaqut in very
expressive terms. Says the author, " the Queen was aware that
her attitude towards Yaqut had created jealousy among the
other Amirs. But what could she do? Being human, she
needed to relax now and then, especially when the cares of state
exhausted her. It was different when Altunia was in Delhi;
he had filled the vacuum; but he was now the governor of
Bhatinda—far away from the capital. Yaqut therefore became
almost a habit with her ".

* यथा स्त्रीणां तथा वाचां साधुत्वे दुर्जनो जन: ।

Here is another aspect of the Queen's character as depicted by the author: "Though decisive by nature, she found herself utterly helpless in face of this important problem of her life. It made her more unhappy, adding to the pangs of her loneliness. She tried, consequently, to suppress personal frustration by concentrating on her work more and more. This effort to forget her problem did not however always succeed. Yaqut and she faced this problem together. She said to Yaqut, "I don't know. I am so confused. Frankly I am as fond of Altunia as I am of you. But the two of you move me differently. I cannot tear myself away from either of these attachments". The unsophisticated Yaqut was perplexed and said: "Your Majesty, you cannot love two persons at one and the same time." The woman in Razia helplessly explained: "I am not sure of the morality of my feelings. Perhaps you are right in saying that I should be more decisive. O, Yaqut, I am so confused. Tell me, am I doing something terribly wrong?" This delicately realistic characterisation of the inner feelings of Razia who, with all her achievements as a progressive Queen remains human, shows the gift of the author who has been able to capture the depth of the crisis that Razia faced throughout her life.

As I have already indicated Dr. Zakaria has not written this story merely for the pleasure of narrating the history of Razia and her rule. He has a purpose in mind and the purpose is to focus our attention on the nature of the progressive policies Razia followed throughout the period of her reign. To begin with, she had to face the travails of being a woman. It was the obstinate unwillingness of the nobles to recognise the wisdom of Iltutmish's will making his daughter Razia as his successor which introduced the tragic interlude of six months' rule of Razia's brother. The obstinacy of the nobles was born of their conviction that a woman cannot be a ruler of the people. In that context, the Sultan told the Nizamul Mulk: "You forget that you are born of a woman. The position of a woman in Islam is so high that our Prophet has said that paradise lies at the feet of a woman." When Razia ultimately succeeded to the throne, the Nizamul Mulk repeated the same plea before her though diplomatically and in another form: "women are so gentle and weak; they need to be protected." Razia reacted sharply, "Protected against whom?", she asked: "against your fellow men? You want us to wear a veil—*purdah*—but why should you subject us to such humiliation when the sin does not lie in us but in the eyes of men? Instead of our faces, your eyes and your minds should be veiled."

Razia wanted to abolish the Jazziah or the tax on the *Zimmi* or non-Muslims. Naturally her proposal met with stout opposition from the nobles of the court. In trying to meet their opposition, Razia said, "Religion cannot be understood in parts; it must be taken as a whole. Its spirit is more important than its texts. Do you know that the Prophet once warned, 'Beware!' On the day of judgment I shall myself be the complainant against him who wrongs a *Zimmi* or lays on him a responsibility greater than he can bear or deprives him of anything that belongs to him."

Razia wanted to appoint an Indian Muslim convert from Hinduism, Imamuddin Rayhan as the *Wakif-i-Dar*, an important office, until then held by Turks. That again raised a 'wave' of loud protest. On this occasion, Razia pleaded that though Rayhan was an Indian, he was a Muslim and all Muslims are brothers according to the Quran. But this plea also failed. Razia ultimately yielded because she said she had no desire to displease the Amirs on a matter like that. She thought the bond of Islam was strong enough for them to accept Rayhan as one of them. But she realised that prejudices die hard and reforms had to proceed by slow stages.

On the problem of relationship between Hindus and Muslims in those days, the author has put very wise thoughts in Razia's mouth. "You are wrong, Balban," she said. "The fault lies with us, not with them. Our whole approach towards them is unsympathetic. We do not mix with them; we don't share in their joys and sorrows; we are a race apart from them and we take pride in maintaining this separation. We may be the rulers and they the ruled; but why do we want to inculcate fear in them? Why can't we try and bring them nearer to us?"

The idea underlying this statement of Razia is of great significance even today, though the context is different and the position of the two communities has substantially altered. National and emotional integration between the different communities in this country cannot be achieved unless the sense of separateness which rules their affairs is completely obliterated. The Mussalmans of India must develop a sense of participation in the national life and this sense can be created only if all of us,

Hindus and others, mix with the Muslim community, talk to or with them, and not at them; understand their sentiments and their feelings and share in their sorrows and their joys; their apprehensions and their hopes. That is the message which the author obviously intends to convey by the words he has put in the mouth of Razia. Social contact on friendly intimate terms and a determination to understand each other's point of view and make the necessary adjustments required to bring all of us together is the basic need of social and emotional integration. That is what Razia attempted to do. Evidently she was far ahead of her times and contemporary society was not able either to appreciate her ideas fully or to absorb them in any manner. That, however, is another matter.

Dr. Zakaria has described how Razia wanted to introduce many reforms in social and economic fields during her time. As a true historian, he has not concealed or disguised the fact that some of the attempts made by the Queen did not succeed. The lesson which Dr. Zakaria wants the readers to draw is plain. In order to make socio-economic revolution successful, it is not enough that the ruler issues a fiat or the government of the day passes appropriate orders. Radical changes in the social structure and economic life of the community presuppose that the public conscience must be educated. Age-old beliefs in religious tenets and conservative concepts based on tradition which concern socio-economic matters die very hard. The rigidity of tradition in such matters has to be conquered by the process of slow, secular, consistent and dedicated education. Education of the public mind can transform the traditional outlook of the community and sponsor and foster a proper sense of values in the minds of the average citizens. When education achieves this task, it becomes easier for government to step in and assist the process of socio-economic progress. This position was as true in Razia's time as it is today, and that to my mind is the central theme of this part of Dr. Zakaria's narrative.

The manner in which Razia met with her death has also been described by the author in a very poignant manner. After her marriage with Altunia, the couple lived together for some time. After she spent her night for the first time with Altunia outside the prison walls she woke up with a sense of glorious morning: " There was the same aristocratic tone of voice and accent which was so habitual with the Queen; but the upsurge of new emotions had somewhat changed the expression on her face, which began to show the same splendour as before. Relaxed and much less disturbed, she felt lifted and impelled by an inner rhythm, with fresh—albeit soft and subdued—music playing in her heart." This is a very moving description of a tender moment in the life of Razia.

Contrast with this the poignancy of the last moment of her life; she, Altunia and their army bravely fought a strong and formidable army; in the end both died a warrior's death on the battle-field. As the author puts it, "Razia was asked to surrender, but she refused. What was there for her to live for? Everything she stood for had crumbled before her very eyes. From a distance she saw Altunia engaged in an equally desperate situation. He was also asked to surrender and was promised pardon. For a moment he hesitated—but one look at Razia, and a new defiance gripped him. He fought back and was killed. As his wife, Razia felt elevated. By the manner of his dying he had washed away his sins. It was a moment of glory. She bowed her head in gratitude to God. Finally an arrow struck her in the heart and she collapsed and died instantly." The pathos of the moment and its grandeur and majesty have been fully captured by Dr. Zakaria in his inimitable style.

Razia, whom the author has painted with the skill of an artist, dominates the story. A very cultured person, she was a warm patron of the learned, being herself deeply interested in every branch of knowledge. She gave a new dynamism to the intellectual development of the different races of her vast empire. She established schools, academies, research centres and public libraries where the works of the great philosophers of former times were studied side by side with the Quran and the Traditions of the Prophet. The Hindu treatises on sciences, philosophy, astronomy and literature were also given special recognition and included in the various courses in schools and colleges. Razia always insisted that it was no shame to acknowledge and assimilate truth from whatever source it came, for truth indeed, was universal and all-embracing. It is such a wise, forward looking, progressive Razia who met a glorious death on the battle-field. At that time she was not even thirty years of age, and "with her died a woman of fascinating intellect, vibrant energy and mighty determination, who in a man's world—brought some relief from man's inhumanity to man, upheld the principles of decency in public life and raised higher the torch of civilisation in a mediæval age ".

I have great pleasure in writing this foreword to *Razia: Queen of India.* I have no doubt that all its readers will be fascinated by the book and will be happy to share with Dr. Zakaria his warm enthusiasm for the subject of the story and his passionate belief in the basic concepts for which Razia stood and which constitute articles of faith with the author himself.

20 July 1966   P. B. GAJENDRAGADKAR

PREFACE

IN the midst of the dynastic revolutions and fratricidal wars which characterised the rule of the Sultans of Delhi, Razia stands out as a monumental figure, facing odds with a courage and determination that have earned her a name and fame. An image of her masterly personality, the fearful circumstances under which she came to the throne and the palace intrigues of the period, engineered by the Mamlukes and Amirs, have been pictured by the historians of the period, Minhaj, the author of *Tabakat-i-Nasiri*, Sadruddin Hasan Nizami, the author of *Tajul Ma'aasir*, and Fakhri-Mudabbir, the author of *Bahrul-Ansab*, and of the manuscripts *Adab-ul Harb*, which is kept in the British Museum. It is no easy task to draw material from these sources and portray an unbiased and objective picture of the personality and masterly activity of the Queen. For one thing, no historian worth the name can be expected to write hard facts without being influenced by personal and environmental prejudices. Further, the angle of approach of each may vary according to his own idiosyncracies and predilections which are only human. Judged in this light, no picture of a historic personage, delineated by a contemporary writer, can ever be comprehensive, complete, impartial and objective. All the sources mentioned above must necessarily suffer from normal human imperfections. The sentimental Islamic prejudice against a member of the female sex trying to head an administration was an obsession with all these authors, with the result that the entire approach to the career of Razia was vitiated.

In disentangling the true personality of Razia from such an approach, Dr. Rafiq Zakaria has taken an imaginative and highly interesting attitude to the portrayal of the life and work of the Queen. He has provided a human and sympathetic background to the circumstances leading to the enthronement of Razia. In his picturesque setting of the various scenes, beginning with the one where the dying Iltutmish convenes a meeting of the Mamlukes to discuss the question of his will, Dr. Zakaria has demonstrated a literary flourish, which is as flowing as it is realistic. He has put in the mouth of the Queen a series of logical and

cornering arguments culled out from the Holy Book of Islam
and from accepted Islamic Traditions, which baffled the most
intelligent of the slaves. Human as she was, Razia found an
intelligent partner in Altunia; but Altunia could hardly make
an amorous approach to her. As Dr. Zakaria observes, " Often
he tried to make her lose herself in the ecstasies of an intimate
human relationship; but he could not succeed. There was something inexplicable about her, which held her back. Whatever
it be, Razia would not let her emotions have the better of her."
In fact, she looked a novel figure, perhaps misborn a woman.
She did not inherit or imbibe the natural characteristics of one
of her sex, either because she had little close contact with the
women of the harem or because she was too much preoccupied
with the affairs of the state even in the days of her father's rule.
To quote the author's words: " Consequently she was surrounded
by men and grew up untutored in the ways of a woman. This
inculcated in her, no doubt, a feeling of equality with men, but
in the process she lost something—that peculiar submissiveness
of a woman which would be equally effective against men."

This appraisal of Razia's peculiarities and uncommon characteristics, which precipitated the crisis of loyalty, is that which
makes the author's approach singularly and agreeably his own.
No woman other than Razia would ever remark, " I am wondering about human relationships. You see I am happy because I
am a woman, but perhaps I would be still happier if there were
no men around to trouble women. They demand everything
from us, but what do they give us in return? Love, they say.
Selfish creatures! They do not know the meaning of the word."
Such sentiments add to the dignity and nobility of the royal
lady. Her unselfish devotion to the cause of the empire, her
eagerness to meet her subjects and mix freely with them, her
tolerance of her co-religionists and her intense practical outlook
in life were more the objects of adverse criticism than of com-
mendation by the Muslim historians. In fact, in the light of
slender evidence, the historians draw unwarranted conclusions,
at times extremely damaging to the personality of the Queen;
that is how Razia's infatuation for Altunia, her military valour,
and the manner of her death have come in for unpleasant and
unjustifiable comment.

The author of this monograph, Dr. Zakaria, has found time,
in the midst of his political pre-occupations, to study these origi-

nal sources, mainly *Tabakat-i-Nasiri*, and gather his facts about the career of Razia. Obviously the inadequate justice done to her by these sources should have warranted the decision of the author to extricate the Queen from the clutches of these biased criticisms and to outline her history with a vividness of description characteristic of an artist.

The monograph contains sixteen chapters, dealing with the entire career of the Queen. It is no dry-as-dust chronicle of prosaic facts but reads like a historical novel, centering round the Queen with whose highest qualities are contrasted those of Shah Turkan, an inhuman and ruthless demon. The book begins with the last days of Sultan Shamsuddin Iltutmish, when, at his death bed, he held a council of Amirs and left a will, leaving the Sultanate to his daughter Razia; then it goes on to deal with the plot of the Amirs ending in the enthronement of Ruknuddin and the machination of Shah Turkan to kill Razia. Chapter 5 outlines Shah Turkan's horrible plot to kill Razia, and how it failed. In Chapters 6 and 7 the arrest and execution, after trial, of Ruknuddin and Shah Turkan, and the coronation of Razia are described. The benevolent measures of Razia and her catholic outlook created suspicion among Amirs who began to plot against her. It is here that the author depicts the cultural tastes and the regal delights of the Queen. In Chapter 12 is described the opposition headed by Balban gaining ground and the Amirs massing support against her, attributing her fondness for the Abyssinian Yaqut to ulterior motives. The last four chapters deal with widespread revolts against her, which culminated in her death.

The author feels that Razia's brief rule of three and a half years was a turning point in the dark history of the period, though the mature results of her good measures hardly outlived her. The author says in his Epilogue, " The Razia that is emerging from the preceding pages is as real as any historical figure of that era; but she is as much the product of the historical material as of the urge within my own breast ". He has recreated the achievements of the Queen in the living thought of the present and has drawn upon imagination and sympathy to bring back to life her " unique characteristics instead of enshrining them in dry-as-dust categories of philosophy ".

A biography which is the outcome of an inward urge to render justice to a victimised historical personage is sure to be appreciated. The monograph is a welcome addition to the list of historical biographies. The author has done a very useful service to the cause of history by writing this imaginative study and deserves to be congratulated on his achievement.

Madras   K. A. NILAKANTA SASTRI
10th July 1966

ACKNOWLEDGMENTS

In the preparation and writing of this book I am indebted to many—some, whom I regard as personal friends and who allowed me the benefit of discussion with them; some others, whose valuable works, as listed in the bibliography, proved of invaluable benefit and enlightenment to me; and still others, my seniors in age and scholarship, who encouraged and guided me in my task. To mention them all is not possible; but I will be failing in my duty if I did not express my deep sense of gratitude to Dr. P. B. Gajendragadkar, the former Chief Justice of India and one of the intellectual giants of modern India for his brilliant and scintillating Foreword; to Prof. K. A. Nilakanta Sastri, Emeritus Professor of History at the University of Madras, a recipient of Padma Bhushan and one of our greatest living historians, for his scholastic Preface; to Prof. H. K. Sherwani, an acknowledged authority on the early Muslim period of India, and a highly respected historian who was honoured with the Presidentship of the Silver Jubilee session of the Indian History Congress, for his encouragement; to Mr. A. S. Raman, the well-known editor of the *Illustrated Weekly of India,* for the keen interest that he took in my work and for having serialised it in his esteemed journal; and to Mr. Shiavax Chavda for his exquisite line drawings, which bring out vividly the feel and environment of the times.

I am also grateful to my old friend Mr. T. K. Seshadri, the News Editor of the *Economic Times,* who had so ably helped me in my earlier work *A Study of Nehru,* and who gave me the benefit of many valuable suggestions for this book; likewise I thank Mr. R. P. Iyer, a free lance journalist of long standing and Mr. R. Gopalkrishna of the *Illustrated Weekly of India.*

To Prof. John Correia-Afonso, Director of the world-famous Father Heras Institute of Indian History, I must extend my thanks for the interest he took in my work and the help he gave me.

To my personal staff, in particular, Mr. D. L. Murudkar, Mr. M. D. Prabhawalkar and Mr. S. Y. P. Quadri, I must offer my grateful thanks for the pains they took, while the work was under preparation, and for the tedium of typing and retyping the manuscripts.

Mr. Ramdas Bhatkal of Popular Prakashan has given me great understanding. I regard him as one of our most enlightened publishers and thank him sincerely for the interest he took in this publication.

And lastly to my wife, I owe the deepest debt of gratitude for, without her, this book would not have seen the light of the day.

28th August 1966   RAFIQ ZAKARIA

PART ONE

THE ACCOUNT

—Quia mihi pulchrum in primis videtur non pati occidere.

I hold it a noble task to rescue from oblivion those who deserve to be eternally remembered.

—PLINY THE YOUNGER
Epistles, Bk. V, epis. 8

1

THE TESTAMENT OF ILTUTMISH

IT was the year 1236.

The Mongols under the leadership of Ogdai Khan, the son of the great Jengis Khan, had swept right across Asia to Russia. Theirs was, indeed, an amazing march, which shook the whole world. In less than six years they had overrun Poland and occupied Hungary. Nearer in Asia, the Kin empire was already subdued, the supremacy of the Sung rulers challenged, the Kingdoms of Khorasan and Persia annexed, their glorious centres of art and culture such as Bokhara, Balkh, Merv, Samarkand, and Nishapur and Tashkent looted, and the frontiers of India threatened and pierced. The Mongols were nomads, riding their wiry horses from pasture to pasture, fishing and hunting for their food and sleeping in tents, come winter, come rain; but their valour was incomparable, their military strategy impeccable and their genius for leadership and organisation unsurpassed. For them natural impediments hardly existed; neither nations nor empires could withstand their terrible thrust. They expected little mercy from their enemies; they showed none. Theirs was a restless spirit, which hungered for victory; it was this spirit which enabled both

Jengis and Ogdai to embark upon a series of conquests which rank among the greatest in all history.

At this time there ruled in Delhi Sultan Shamsuddin Iltutmish. He was an able king, who had somehow managed by tact and diplomacy to check the Mongol hordes, threatening the outskirts of his kingdom. He had been ruler for 26 years and his empire extended from Prashar in the extreme north-west to the river Brahmaputra in Bengal and to the extremities of Gujarat and Orissa nearer south. A man of unusual vigour, he succeeded his master, Qutbuddin Aibak, known as the founder of the Slave Dynasty in the annals of mediæval India. Like Aibak, Iltutmish was also a slave. He was bought by Aibak himself, according to some historians, in the bàzars of Ghaznin; according to some others, in the streets of Delhi.

In his *Tabakat-i-Nasiri*, Minhajus Seraj narrates that Iltutmish was of high and noble origin but had been betrayed and sold like Joseph by his jealous and unkind brothers or nephews to some merchants and taken to Bokhara. They had sold him there to other merchants who, in turn, had sold him to yet others, until he was brought back to Ghaznin. However, by then he was so highly priced that it became difficult to obtain a buyer. Finally, Aibak heard of him, paid the price, and brought him to Delhi.

However that be, Iltutmish came to Delhi as a slave. He soon gained the confidence of his master, who treated him as a son. He rose rapidly, becoming eventually the governor of the province of Badaun. On Aibak's death, his son Aram managed the affairs of the empire for some time; but the final selection had to be made by the Forty Amirs—the powerful group of Turkish nobles, who had emerged as a decisive factor in the body politic of the empire. They decided upon Iltutmish, though their

choice was by no means unanimous. The support of
the commander-in-chief of the armed forces, Sipah Salar
Ali Ismail, who was also the Amir-i-Dad of Delhi, turned
the scales in favour of Iltutmish; he was also favoured
by the chief justice and blessed by the *ulema* or religious
leaders.

The opposition was led by the powerful Sar-Jandar,
the head of the bodyguards; he was supported by some
Amirs, who wanted Aibak's son, Aram, to be confirmed
as the successor. For some time tension prevailed and
there was a small but fierce rising of the *jandars* (bodyguards) in support of Aram, but ultimately the succession of Iltutmish was accepted by the Forty Amirs. It
was a good choice for the new ruler had qualities which
put him head and shoulders above Aram and the others.
He was bold, able, shrewd and, withal, amiable. He
knew the art of winning friends. Though ambitious,
he was careful not to overreach himself. In his hands,
his compatriots believed, the empire would be safe. He
had an imposing personality, tall and serene, a long sensitive face, an aquiline nose, and a leonine voice. He was
every inch a king.

Iltutmish lived up to the expectations of his friends;
as the years rolled on he grew in stature. But he had
to work hard. The throne of Delhi was no bed of roses;
to preserve it he had to fight many wars, big and small,
now against his own kith and kin, now against the dis-
gruntled Amirs, now against the Hindu Rajas, who often
revolted against foreign domination and, in some cases,
succeeded in re-establishing their authority.

One of the last expeditions that Iltutmish led was to
suppress the rebellion that had broken out at Bonian, a
place somewhere in the hilly tracts of the Sind-Sagar
Doab; its suppression proved a tough and strenuous
affair and exhausted the Sultan considerably. He was,

nevertheless, happy and felt grateful to Allah for his benevolence. As was his habit on such occasions, he remembered his saint, the great Qutbuddin Bakhtiar al-Kaki, to whom he ascribed all his good fortune. In his memory he constructed the magnificent Qutb Minar—that beautiful column in Delhi, which is still one of the wonders of the world. He gave it the necessary spiritual touch by making it in the form of a minaret, tall and majestic, so that it might not only remind the world of his age and glory but also of the spiritual greatness of the saint.

On his way back to the palace, the Sultan told his Prime Minister—the Nizamul Mulk, as he was called—Muhammad Junaidi, that he would like to halt for some time near the Qutb Minar.

" But, Your Majesty," said the Nizamul Mulk, " you are tired and not keeping well. The sooner you reach the palace and rest, the better, Sire."

" You are right, Nizamul Mulk," replied the sovereign. " But I cannot forget my teacher in my hour of victory. However tired, I must pay my reverence to his memory. It was he who taught me the true meaning of life. No, Nizamul Mulk, I must stop for a while near his column, say my *maghrib* (evening) prayers there and then return to the palace."

The sun was about to set; the sky had darkened; but for the troops there were hardly any people in the street; only the sound of the hoofs of the horses broke the silence. As the troops neared the column, they halted. The Sultan then dismounted.

He did *wazu* (ablutions) and led the prayers. Then he visited the tomb of al-Kaki and bowed before his grave, remembering the days when he came to Delhi as a slave, the various struggles he had passed through, the battles he had fought, the governorships he had held, and finally the Crown! It all seemed a dream and still how true it was. He had faced many trials and tribulations but with every success had come temptations. Sometimes Iltutmish had succumbed to these, but often he had risen above them, mainly because of the influence of al-Kaki, who had taught him many of the virtues of life. On becoming emperor, Iltutmish had offered al-Kaki the position of Shaikh-ul-Islam or leader of Islam, which, with characteristic humility, the saint had declined, for he was indeed a man of God, above want and desire.

Before resuming his journey, the Sultan looked once again at the Qutb Minar, admired its workmanship—in particular the grandeur of its height and the tracery of Quranic inscriptions with which it was adorned. It was an exquisite expression in stone and mortar of the depth of the emperor's feelings for Qutbuddin al-Kaki; a mere look at the column gave the royal disciple a peculiar spiritual solace.

On reaching the palace, the usual formalities were shortened and the Sultan immediately retired to his bed-chamber. He was received by the proud and self-assured Shah Turkan, formerly the chief of the concubines but whom he had married on the death of his master, Qutbuddin Aibak. The ladies in attendance were ordered to leave. The Sultan desired to be left alone with his former mistress, now the Malika, who, by her charm and brilliance, had acquired a unique hold on the aged ruler; he liked her straw-coloured complexion, her green eyes, her voluptuous and well-preserved figure and the acquired coquettishness which made her one of the most glamorous ladies of the realm.

Resting on his bed, the Sultan told Shah Turkan of his victory, but at the same time confided in her that he was feeling weak and worn out. She enquired whether the royal physician should be summoned.

"Presently, my dear wife," said the Sultan, "but first I must decide about the succession."

"The succession!" cried Shah Turkan. "But why should you talk of succession? May your enemies die and may your shadow always protect us!"

"All of us have to die, Shah Turkan," he said. "As the Quran says: 'All living things have to taste death.' As over our birth so over our death we have no control. Don't be upset, my Malika. You must be ready for all eventualities. Just send for Tajuddin."

Tajuddin was the Sultan's secretary of state, whom he had selected, as a promising young man in the early years of his rule and given one higher position after another, ultimately entrusting him with one of the most coveted offices in the Sultanate. Now middle-aged, he was more a scholar than a politician. Sober and subdued, Tajuddin dressed simply and neatly and spoke in a well-modulated and soft voice. There was something about his bearing which compelled respect. A person of infinite loyalty and compassion, he was an epitome of the civilised life. He was, however, not enough of a man of action. He lacked initiative, though not ideas. Living in his ivory tower, he remained cut off from the labyrinth of palace intrigues.

In a few moments Tajuddin arrived. The Sultan talked to him for a while and then asked him to take down his will. Tajuddin obeyed. Under it he appointed his daughter, Razia, as his successor.

Shah Turkan was aghast. She could not contain herself.

"But how can you do such a thing?" she burst out.

"Why not?" the Sultan retorted. "Have you forgotten that I am the Sultan?"

"Forgive me, my lord, for my impertinence. But what about our sons?" asked Shah Turkan.

"I had only one son—Nasiruddin Mahmud—a good, intelligent, brave man; but he is dead."

"What about Ruknuddin, Sire?" she anxiously enquired.

"Shah Turkan, I know he is your son. But so is he mine. And he is our eldest. My affection for him is no less than yours. I wish I could have made him my successor. But you know what he is—a profligate, a drunkard, a debauchee. How can I leave the kingdom in his charge? He will ruin it."

"Please do not be so unkind, my master," she said. "You can train him to be worthy of you."

"What do you think I have been doing all these years? And with what result? No, Shah Turkan, our son is no good. He is incapable of being a ruler. He will be a pawn in the hands of others. Your other son is no better. Both of them are given to ease and pleasure. And let me tell you frankly, I blame you for it. My only son who has the qualities of kingship in him is Qutbuddin. But he is just a boy. I have no choice but to appoint Razia. What do you say, Tajuddin?"

"As you please, Sire. I appreciate the reasons that have compelled you to take this decision. I believe it is a good decision, which will strengthen the foundations of the empire."

"I knew you would understand, Tajuddin, but I am not sure about my other Amirs. Prejudice dies hard. They will resent the fact that Razia is a woman. I have no strength to argue with them. Hence I charge you to keep the will a secret. It is to be opened only after my death and read out to the durbar."

Shah Turkan was dumbfounded. She could not imagine that the Sultan would be so deaf to her pleadings. He assured her that Razia would look after her and protect her interests; but the Malika feared for the future. The loss of her husband would be bad enough; but what was to follow would be much worse. There was no love lost between Razia and Shah Turkan; it was too late now for any good understanding between them.

2

SECRET BETRAYED

As the days passed, the Sultan's condition became worse; the physicians in attendance gave up hope. The end was near.

Shah Turkan became desperate; she did not know what to do. What would become of her if Razia ascended the throne? She was worried. The exalted position which she had so long enjoyed could not last. Soon she would have neither power nor influence. Both her sons were weaklings; they were devoid of tact and ability—especially the eldest and her favourite, Ruknuddin Firoz, had none of the qualities of a king. The more she pondered over the problem, the more gloomy appeared the prospects. But she could not just keep quiet; she had to act before the situation became hopeless.

Shah Turkan reflected on the matter for a few days and then decided that she must divulge the secret of the Sultan's will to the Amirs: in doing so, she, no doubt, took a great risk. The Sultan might divorce her; he might banish her; he might even hang her. But what was the alternative? She could not sit back and watch the power she had gained after so many years' hard and bitter struggle slipping from her hands.

At last she asked for the Nizamul Mulk. He was an old man, with an authoritarian outlook. Orthodox and

unbending, he could be extremely narrow in his
approach. Though clever and resourceful, he feared to
tread a new path; for him only the beaten track. He
came dressed in his regal garb, walking leisurely, not
sensing in the least the seriousness of the occasion. Shah
Turkan told him all about the will, dramatising the
development for the desired effect. The old man was
shocked.

"But how can His Majesty do such a thing?" he exclaimed. "It will disrupt the empire."

"I know!" said Shah Turkan, pleased with his reaction. "That is why I have taken the risk of betraying his secret to you. If His Majesty comes to know of my action, he will never forgive me."

"But I cannot keep it a secret, Your Majesty," said the Nizamul Mulk. "I must divulge it to the Amirs. I know they will not welcome Razia's nomination; in fact they will rebel. But whatever be the risk, some of us must see the Sultan immediately and try to dissuade him from such a course of action."

"You may do, Nizamul Mulk," she replied, "whatever you deem proper in the interests of the empire, but please see that no harm comes to me. After all I am only doing my duty."

"That is so, Your Majesty," said the Nizamul Mulk. "You may rest assured that the Amirs and I would do our best to see that you do not suffer in the process."

So saying the Nizamul Mulk rushed to his office and summoned the powerful Forty Amirs, who were subsequently to make and unmake kings. Most of them reacted sharply. They were unhappy at the Sultan's choice. There were some among them, though, who tried to argue for Razia and said that in view of the worthlessness of the two elder sons, the daughter's nomination was inevitable. The most conspicuous of them was the young, impetuous Amir Altunia, who had been a playmate of Razia. Handsome, well-built, and strong-willed, but rather petulant and restless, he was still a junior in the Turkish hierarchy. His advocacy of Razia had a selfish tinge. The two were known friends; they shared many things in common. Young and ambitious, both belonged to a different generation, and they had a new vision of the empire as a beehive of reform and radicalism.

However, Altunia had yet to make his mark; little heed was therefore paid by the elders to what he said. They also decided that some of them should seek an audience with the Sultan and wait in deputation on him.

The audience was fixed for the same evening. Some ten Amirs, led by the Nizamul Mulk, saw the Sultan. At first, they were rather nervous; they hesitated to talk; but the Sultan put them immediately at ease.

"I know why you have come, my Amirs," said the Sultan. "I also know who has betrayed my secret to you; but I am too old now to punish people. God will take care of them. But I ask you if you should allow yourself to be persuaded by a woman who could not remain loyal to her husband even in the evening of his life."

"Please forgive us, Your Majesty; but the Malika also owed a duty to the empire."

"You know as well as I do, Nizamul Mulk," said the Sultan, reproachingly, "that it was no call of duty which made her do such a disloyal act. It was the fear of the loss of her hold on the court." He added, with some annoyance, "Whatever that be, I shall deal with the Malika in my own way; now tell me what is bothering you."

"The nomination, Your Majesty," submitted the Nizamul Mulk.

"And what is wrong with the nomination?" demanded the Sultan.

"Your Majesty, Princess Razia is a woman. How can we give allegiance to a woman?" said the Nizamul Mulk humbly but with apparent anxiety.

" Why can't you? There have been women who have graced the throne in the past. Take Iran. The great Khusrau Parvez was succeeded one after the other by his two daughters—Purandukht and Arjumandukht. And that was many centuries ago. I hope we have progressed since then!"

" Please understand our susceptibilities, Your Majesty," pleaded the Nizamul Mulk. " The Princess may prove to be an enlightened ruler; but we have all grown up under different traditions in this foreign land. It is difficult for us to submit to the will of a woman."

" You forget, Nizamul Mulk, that you are born of a woman. The position of a woman in Islam is so high that our Prophet has said that paradise lies at the feet of a woman."

" Forgive me, Your Majesty, but the saying goes: ' Paradise lies at the feet of the mother '," said the Nizamul Mulk, humbly and respectfully.

" But isn't a mother a woman?" demanded the Sultan.

" That is so, my lord," replied the Nizamul Mulk. " But the affairs of a kingdom are a different proposition. I submit most humbly that these cannot be managed by a woman; she is meant for the home. There are so many natural handicaps from which she suffers; she will not be able to control the Amirs."

" Or is it because you fear that she will be able to control them too well?" thundered the Sultan.

The Amirs became frightened; the Nizamul Mulk lost his nerve. Another powerful Amir, the long-moustached, heavy and powerful-looking Malik Izzuddin Ayaz, intervened. " Please do not misunderstand us, our Master," he told the Sultan. " We have the highest esteem for Razia; we know of her great qualities of head and heart."

The Sultan interrupted, "And have you forgotten how she always assisted me in the affairs of my kingdom? What an excellent administrator she made when I entrusted her with the affairs of the empire in Delhi during my absence in Gwalior!"

"Of course we all know it, Your Majesty. And we have nothing but the greatest admiration for her," admitted Ayaz. "But this is a much bigger responsibility; it is a much more onerous task. We wish Razia were your son, not your daughter; she has everything, Sire, but the right sex."

"I don't agree with you, Ayaz," observed the Sultan. "Neither our religion nor the interest of the empire allows us to indulge in such discrimination. Turkish history is also full of instances where women were chosen as rulers instead of men. What about the rule of the widow of Gur Khan and his daughter Koyuwk Khatun? In Halab, in North Mesopotamia, Safia Khatun reigned for some time. And don't you remember the rule of that beautiful slave girl, Shajarat al-Durr, who succeeded the Memeluke Sultan Ayub to the throne of Egypt? The nobles of that ancient land accepted her unanimously."

"That is true, our Lord, but the situation in India is different; we are strangers here and we must be careful," implored Ayaz.

"Not careful," said the Sultan, "but more responsive to the needs of the empire. That is why I am appointing Razia. I am not appointing her because she is a woman. I am appointing her because she alone can manage the affairs of the state and hold the empire together. As you have rightly said, she has everything. She is young; despite her beauty she knows how to carry herself; she has poise and dignity; she is dynamic; she is full of ideas. And unlike my two elder sons she is

not given to a life of ease and comfort. Her character
is unimpeachable; her behaviour, exemplary. In learning she has no equal at the court. She can manage
with distinction both the spoken and written word. She
has command over the Arabic language. She is well
versed in the Quran and the traditions of the Prophet
of Islam. What more do you want?"

" That is all true, Your Majesty, but. . . ."

" I am afraid," interrupted the Sultan with some irrita-
tion, "you must reconcile yourselves to my desire.
Razia has been the light of my eyes; I want her to be
the light of my empire."

" Does our opinion mean nothing to you, Sire?" asked
Ayaz sulkingly.

" Aren't you being unfair to me?" said the Sultan.
" You have been my trusted counsellors; but on this issue
I feel you are wrong. Believe me, my Amirs, if you want
me to die in peace and the kingdom to remain intact
then Razia must succeed me."

Disappointed, the Amirs, one by one, made their
obeisance and left the Sultan's bed-chamber.

A few days later, on April 29, 1236, the Sultan
breathed his last, mourned, on the one hand, by his
Amirs and Maliks, who respected him for his military
conquests, and, on the other, by his thousands of soldiers,
who loved him for having given them a comfortable
habitation in a foreign land. His subjects, irrespective
of race and creed, also felt his loss, for his long rule had
provided them with a sense of security achieved not only
by the welding together of loosely-conquered territories
into a political unity but also by the tactful warding off
of a likely onslaught by the Mongols which would have
resulted in untold death and destruction. A protector
of the public weal, he had guarded the highways,
encouraged trade and commerce and given immediate

relief to his subjects during famines. Prone to flattery, and at times cruel and ruthless, he still had his head on his shoulders. He was, indeed, the greatest of the Slave Kings to have sat on the throne of Delhi. His passing, therefore, created a terrible void; it proved both an opportunity and a challenge to the Forty Amirs.

3

THE TRIUMPH OF MANHOOD

Soon after the death of the Sultan, as charged by him, his loyal secretary of state, Tajuddin, summoned the Court of Amirs to declare formally the wish of the Sultan in regard to his successor. Present on the occasion, apart from the Nizamul Mulk and the Amirs, were Shah Turkan and her two sons Ruknuddin and Ghiasuddin. There were, besides, the late Sultan's youngest son, by another wife, Qutbuddin, still in his teens, and Razia, the princess, who, though simply dressed, was the cynosure of all eyes. Her slender figure, jet-black hair and brown-coloured eyes, the sheen of her skin, which seemed a mixture of lily and rose, and, above all, the majesty of her face and the beauty of her expression created a halo round her personality, which could not fail to impress the gathering.

In many respects Razia was like the picture painted by Firdausi, in his *Shahnama*, of the emperor's daughter Tahmineh, whom the great warrior Rustam married:

Clear as the moon in glowing charms arrayed,
Her winning eyes the light of heaven displayed;
Her cypress form entranced the gazer's view;
Her waving curls, the heart, resistless drew;

Her eyebrows like the Archer's bended bow;
Her ringlets, snares; her cheek, the rose's glow
Mixed with the lily;—from her ear-tips hung
Rings rich and glittering, star-like; and her tongue
And tips sugared sweetness;—pearls the while
Sparkled within a mouth formed to beguile;
Her presence dimmed the stars and breathing round—
Fragrance and joy, she scarcely touched the ground:
So light her step, so graceful—every part
Perfect, and suited to her spotless heart.

Tajuddin read out the will; it caused a commotion among the Amirs. The Nizamul Mulk stood up and said, " Though we loved our Sultan and had always been loyal to him, I am of the opinion that Razia's accession to the throne will create much trouble. Neither the Amirs nor the governors of the provinces are willing to accept a woman as their ruler."

" But, Nizamul Mulk," reminded Tajuddin, " you had told all this to our gracious sovereign; and yet he willed that he should be succeeded by Razia."

" Yes," said the Nizamul Mulk sharply, " but His Majesty was too ill to understand the intricacies of the situation; nor would it have been right for us to bother him too much, knowing as we did the state of his health."

" But he was firm on his decision," intervened Altunia. " He had refused to alter it, even after your pleadings."

" Young man," rebuked the Nizamul Mulk, " there is more than meets the eye in all such matters; the affairs of the kingdom are still beyond you; you will live and learn."

There was animated talk among the Amirs; they began to argue agitatedly. Suddenly the atmosphere became charged with excitement. Razia sized up the situation and realised that most of the Amirs were against her suc-

cession.   She sat through the whole proceedings without
uttering a word; but she observed one Amir after
another carefully.   And as the commotion mounted, she
stood up, came forward and addressed the gathering.

" My good friends," she said, " and the good friends
of our empire, I understand your apprehensions about
my succession; and I respect you for having expressed
them so openly, frankly and freely.   I admire your

courage. What you have said may not be acceptable to me, but I know that you do not dislike me personally; your objection to my succession arises from your prejudice against my sex. That prejudice is not of recent origin; it goes deep down in human history. For the present what we are concerned with is the unity of our ranks and the preservation of our empire. My succession, in defiance of your declared views, will not serve

either purpose. I have, therefore, decided to abide by your judgment; there should now be an end to this matter. In the interests of the empire, I appeal to all of you to stop the dissension in our ranks. Let us remain united. At this hour of our trial, I am reminded of the words of our Prophet: ' Said he, " Shall I tell you what is better than prayer and fasting and the highest form of charity? It is to resolve internal dissensions and bring about concord between contending parties. It is internal dissension that primarily ruins a society " ' So let us follow his saying and end this dispute. For my part I hereby give my allegiance to my brother, Ruknuddin. May God give him the strength to keep us together and to preserve our empire!"

The Amirs were taken aback; such a development was altogether unexpected. They thought there would be a fight. They burst into rejoicing therefore and hailed Razia as the true friend of the empire. Shah Turkan, who had sat motionless all the time, heaved a sigh of relief; in the midst of all the excitement that Razia's dramatic announcement caused, the Nizamul Mulk proclaimed Ruknuddin the new Sultan. One Amir after another came to him, kissed his hand and expressed his allegiance.

As soon as the durbar was over, Razia retired to her bed-chamber; she was sad and dejected; it was no ordinary matter for her to dishonour the will of her father, whom she had adored. But what could she do in the circumstances? Resistance might have disrupted the empire.

Tired and downcast she told her maid-in-waiting, Parveen, that she should not be disturbed. But hardly had she given the orders, when Altunia arrived. Parveen tried to persuade him not to disturb the princess; but he was insistent. Finally she gave in.

As soon as Razia saw Altunia, she begged of him not to bother her.

"I am in no mood for any talk," she pleaded.

"I know you are tired but I am at a loss to understand why you surrendered. We could certainly have fought them. After all there was the will of the Sultan; the people would have been with us."

"You are a man, Altunia," replied Razia. "But you do not know how deep-rooted is the prejudice among men against women. They want us as their chattels: to look after their homes and to produce their children—nothing more. My father was too advanced—far ahead of his age. As for you, Altunia, you want me to be queen because you love me. I am not sure if your prejudice against women, as such, is any the less."

"Please do not talk like this, my princess," said Altunia caressingly. "True it is that I love you; but that does not mean that I am blind to the realities of the situation.

The fact is that even your worst critics do not doubt your great administrative talents; the Amirs said so to the Sultan. I may be mistaken, but I feel that their opposition is more because of your accomplishments than because you are a woman. They are making a convenient excuse of it to suit their selfish·interests. We cannot be so naive as not to understand their motives. There are many like me in the court who have full faith in you. They may be in a minority, but they are prepared to stand by you regardless of the consequences."

"You are kind, Altunia," said Razia with some softness in her voice. "I am sòrry if I have offended you; it is because of the bitterness that has entered my heart. I know I have some good friends, but we must not precipitate matters; we must wait and watch."

"You do not know how heart-broken and dejected Tajuddin is," said Altunia. "He feels he has betrayed his master."

"Please ask him not to feel disheartened," Razia told Altunia. "There are occasions when discretion must be observed; recklessness is no virtue; our valour should not scorn our senses. Who knows what the future holds in store for us? We must trust in God, for if it is His will that I should be the Sultan, no man can stop it."

"That is our prayer, noble lady."

"Altunia, will you tell Tajuddin on my behalf to compose a poem in honour of the new Sultan on his coronation?"

"That will be hypocrisy; Tajuddin is too self-respecting a person to agree to it."

"I have accepted Ruknuddin as the Sultan. Is it not then the duty of my friends to honour my decision?"

"We do, my princess; but we need not be enthusiastic about it and sing the praises of the new Sultan. Praise must not be mere lip service; it must come deep from the heart; to praise the unworthy is a robbery of the deserving. After all you know that we do not consider your brother to be fit for Kingship."

" Yes, but even so we should not act in a manner which may seem as if we are not sincere in our allegiance to the new Sultan. The interests of the empire demand that our *bona fides* should not be suspect; that will not help the cause of unity."

" But do you really believe that Ruknuddin will rise to the occasion?"

" He may not; the task, in fact, may prove too big for him. But let the Amirs find that out for themselves. I do not propose to create problems for my brother. I sincerely wish that he may rule as long as he can."

" And meanwhile must we act as his slaves?"

" I do not suggest that, Altunia. Because we belong to the family of slaves we have learnt one lesson: never to sacrifice our self-respect."

" But that is what our behaviour would result in."

" Not necessarily, if we do not lose faith in the cause of our empire."

" Do you think in the prevailing atmosphere of murder, corruption and moral degeneration, anyone cares for the cause?"

" But we must; otherwise the empire will go to pieces. I know you love me, Altunia, which perhaps makes you talk so impetuously. But, if we have to overcome the present crisis, then we must have faith in ourselves and in the justice of our cause."

" Aren't all these matters relative to one's own position?"

" No. And the best way of realising it is to ask one's own conscience. Once Abu Amama, a companion of the Prophet of Islam asked him, ' What is faith?' The Prophet answered: ' Whenever a good deed done by you

gives you inward joy and whenever a wrong done by
you gives you a sense of regret, you are verily a man of
faith.' That is the basis of faith; not self-interest, or
pride."

" I am afraid your standards are too high, Razia.
They will not succeed against the present unscrupulous
clique."

" But if we adopt the same methods as they do, what
is the difference, then, between us and them?"

" Time is running against us and you are becoming
more and more philosophical, Razia."

" I don't agree with you, Altunia. Time is in our
favour, but we must have patience."

" Patience! Patience! I am tired of it. I want to
act."

" I appreciate your anxiety, Altunia. But we must
not do anything to disrupt the empire. Nor should we
do anything which would be in the nature of disloyalty
to the throne. That would strike at the very root of our
empire, for it is the throne which stands as the symbol
of our unity."

" Not the throne, as it is occupied now."

" Once we try to intrigue against the throne, whoever
be the occupant and whatever be the reasons, our rule
will not last long. We have to make this throne strong
and sure; a shaky throne is like ice on a hot day."

" But if that is your approach, Ruknuddin can never
be deposed."

" If he is to be deposed, it must be because of his own
actions, not by intrigues on our part."

" The way you look at it, Razia, I don't think we can
ever succeed."

" Tell me, Altunia, are you more interested in me or
in the empire?"

"In both, because the two are inter-dependent, my noble princess."

"Even so, mine is the right approach; it alone will strengthen me and save the empire."

"I hope so, but at present I am all confused."

So were many of Razia's supporters at the court. They were anxious to organise themselves against the new regime and to strike at it; but the princess would not encourage them. She knew that intrigues led to counter-intrigues and once such a process was set in motion it would divide the empire from top to bottom. Razia was eager to avoid it at all costs, for she did not want the kingdom, which her father had built with his sweat and blood, to become a battle-field of warring Turkish Amirs. Statesmanship demanded the exercise of tact and patience and the princess possessed both these qualities in abundance.

4

A SULTAN WHO DID NOT RULE

THE coronation of Ruknuddin provided an occasion for great pomp and pageantry. It was the first event of its kind since the impressive build-up of the Sultanate by Iltutmish and was naturally celebrated on a big scale. The Forty Amirs were there, all in their ceremonial and colourful attire; the governors arrived from the far-flung provinces, with their full retinue; the *ulema* with their flowing beards and in their long robes; the bodyguards presented a memorable sight, in their glittering head-gear and uniforms; the ordinary folks of Delhi also came, dressed in their best. Shah Turkan supervised the arrangements personally; no detail escaped her scrutiny. She looked the proudest person in the whole assembly for she knew that it was more her coronation than that of her son. She moved among the people as if she were the mistress of the realm; dressed in gold and silver and loaded with ornaments, she strutted about as if she were the shadow of God on earth. Mightily pleased with herself, with an aura of self-importance, she gave a cold stare to the ladies of the harem, forgetting her own origin. Only at Razia she dared not look; some strange sense of fear seized her, or was it her guilty conscience? Finally, the Nizamul Mulk read out the declaration and the celebrations began in all their gaiety and mirth.

As desired by Razia, Tajuddin came forward and recited his poem, which he had specially composed for the occasion. A poet of distinction, he was heard with rapt attention. He began:

May the perpetual empire be of omen good,
To the King, specially in his time of youth:
Yamin-ud Dowlah Ruknuddin, who has been crowned,
May his rule be ushered in!

And so it went on; there was praise, but not unqualified. Tajuddin was a master of satire; he had a way with words. Razia admired his virtuosity; she felt grateful to him for having honoured her wish. The poem lacked warmth, but it had the perfectionist's touch. True, Tajuddin did not express his innermost feelings on the occasion and the note of cynicism in his composition was deftly woven; but it glorified the new Sultan as Razia had wanted and invoked the blessings of Allah for his prosperity and long life.

Soon after the coronation, Ruknuddin, with the power and wealth that the kingship offered him, began to amuse himself. He led a life of ease and pleasure. His activities became a matter of public scandal; the new Sultan did not care to hide his mode of living from his subjects. An extrovert and exhibitionist, he played openly with dancing girls and showered his favours on one and all. Fond of wine, he drank to his heart's content— often more than to his heart's content—with the result that many a time he had to be carried to his bedchamber. He rode on his favourite horse, at times even on an elephant, through the streets of Delhi, and spent lavishly on purchases for the inmates of his harem. The merchants flattered his erratic taste and received gifts in return from the Treasury. It was more easy for a beautiful girl to obtain an audience with the King than for a provincial governor, who might have travelled hundreds of miles for the purpose. The result was that the business of state was neglected and flatterers reaped rich harvests. At first the Nizamul Mulk did not mind the

King's indifference, for it gave him freedom of action, but, as the situation worsened and demoralisation gripped the administration, even he became alarmed.   The King was not available for formal occasions; the Amirs had to wait for days before being received in audience; even

the Nizamul Mulk could not have free access to the Sultan.

One day he reproached the Sultan and reminded him that he was the King.

"The less I remember it the better for you, Nizamul Mulk. You run the empire as you like. Leave me to my wine and women."

"It has become a scandal, a public scandal, Your Majesty. It is not good either for you or for the Sultanate."

"Then what do you expect me to do—give up my pleasures and do your pleasure?"

"Your Majesty, the situation is serious. You must behave yourself."

"I am what I am; you and my mother wanted me to be the King. So I am the King. I think you should depose me and make Razia the Queen: she has all the qualities."

"You should not speak like this, Your Majesty. We all want you to be the King, but kingship demands the performance of certain duties and the observance of certain restraints."

"I see. So from my Prime Minister you are now becoming my reformer. I have no time for all this talk. May I beseech you, Nizamul Mulk, not to interfere in my private affairs!"

Frustrated, the Nizamul Mulk rushed to Shah Turkan, but she did not prove of much help. She was too involved in her own importance to bother about her son. In fact she was happy that the Sultan did not engage himself in serious work. That gave her greater control and more power. And she loved nothing better than the exercise of power. Already she had established a reign of terror in the harem; many of its inmates were oppressed; some were even murdered; not a few were banished. Hundreds of others were publicly humiliated, many were reduced to poverty and misery. On the slightest pretext, she took revenge; in the case of those, who had not been friendly with her in the past, she inflicted the severest punishment. Only those who flattered her received her favours; the rest were kept in dread of her.

The Nizamul Mulk was aware of these happenings; but he chose to ignore them. He knew that some of the Amirs were in league with Shah Turkan; she had also many other supporters at the lower level. The Nizamul Mulk's hands were full of problems, which were becoming more and more complicated; he did not want to add to these and make the situation worse.

But the Sultan's behaviour was a different matter; it was spreading disaffection among the people and weakening the imperial structure. The Nizamul Mulk tried to explain the gravity of the situation to Shah Turkan; but it was beyond her comprehension. She never had any political understanding; she lacked vision and foresight. Too drunk with power, she was unable to see the realities of the problem; morally a woman of straw, she cared little for character or integrity.

Feeling utterly hopeless, the Nizamul Mulk began to frighten her; he warned her that if matters were not mended some of the Amirs might depose Ruknuddin and in his place put Qutbuddin on the throne.

"But how can they do it? He is still a boy," demanded Shah Turkan.

"That is exactly the reason why they may do it—so that they may have greater hold on the affairs of the state," explained the Nizamul Mulk.

"You are conspiring against me; I should have known you better—you old rat!" shouted Shah Turkan and

began to curse the Nizamul Mulk and fulminate against
him.

" If it were so, Your Majesty, I would not have warned
you in advance; conspirators do not take their enemies
into confidence.   I am sorry that you have been so unfair
to me; but I claim to be your friend and hence it is my
duty to warn you of what is happening."

" But you are the Prime Minister.   Why don't you
punish those Amirs—banish them?"

" It is easier said than done.   Even the great Iltutmish
could not ignore them; we are much too weak, Shah
Turkan.   But the Amirs dare not misbehave if the Sultan behaves properly.   They must have a cause—and a
very strong cause—for such a disloyal act.   That is why
I beg of you, Your Majesty, to impress upon your son to
lead a more moderate life—at any rate he should not
indulge in his revelries so openly.   Also, he must find
some time to receive the provincial governors; they must
be entertained properly and even humoured by the Sultan—that is the least that kingship demands of him."

Shah Turkan became pensive and then said, " I shall
do my best."   But as soon as the Nizamul Mulk left her,
she began to worry about the prospect of Qutbuddin
becoming the king.   So far she had given him no
thought; all the while it was Razia who had occupied
her mind.   But now she saw in him a new danger.   Her
old hatred of Qutbuddin revived.   He was begotten by
the Sultan of a mistress like her, whom he later married.
For years Shah Turkan had despised both the mother
and the child.   She could not, therefore, bear the
thought that this son of the Sultan, born to her rival,
should rule the kingdom.   Filled with hate and revenge,
she decided to murder Qutbuddin; an innocent child of
hardly ten years, with winning manners and a charming
disposition, he became, hereafter, her obsession.

Shah Turkan did not want to risk a secret plot; she wanted to involve both mother and child openly. So she began accusing the mother—an attractive woman of simple tastes and no ambition—of plotting the murder of the Sultan in order to put her son on the throne. Various situations were created to incriminate her. Even the boy's childlike acts were misinterpreted as seditious. The whole atmosphere was charged with suspicion and fear. Unable to control herself, the poor woman became unbalanced; she began to behave strangely. The boy also became frightened.

Finally Shah Turkan obtained the Sultan's approval— in one of his fits of drunkenness—and put up for trial Qutbuddin and his mother on a charge of sedition against the Sultan. The Nizamul Mulk tried to intervene, cajoled Shah Turkan, pleaded with her, even made use of threats, but all to no avail. Her hand-picked tribunal found both mother and son guilty. The mother was sentenced to be hanged; the son, to be blinded in both his eyes! Even in mediæval times such a travesty of justice had rarely been witnessed. It had a most horrifying effect on the public mind.

5

THE WILES OF SHAH TURKAN

THE news of the horrible developments at the court travelled far and wide; the whole kingdom was in the grip of fear. Delhi presented a spectacle of chaos and anarchy—a scene of decay above and ferment below. Even some of the Amirs lost their nerve; the *ulema* prayed for divine mercy; the bodyguards became restive. The bazars were full of strange, wild rumours and there were whispers all around that something dreadful was brewing at the palace. Those who looked up to the Sultan saw neither will nor light nor decision. Shaken, the Nizamul Mulk summoned the Forty Amirs, who had been equally horrified and no less alarmed by the events. Some of the provincial governors openly talked of establishing separate kingdoms of their own.

Tajuddin rushed to Razia. She alone, he told her, could save the situation. Otherwise, the empire might disintegrate. Razia was, no doubt, perturbed but she was doubtful whether the Amirs would stand by her. Tajuddin felt that the crisis was too grave for anyone to be obstructive and that it could be resolved only by Razia. But the princess was hesitant. She knew how deep-rooted was the prejudice against her; any hasty step might again unite the Amirs in favour of Shah Turkan. And, if that happened, it would further strengthen her hold. Tajuddin argued that Razia had no need to be so cautious; there were moments when risks had to be taken. As the two of them were engrossed in animated discussion, analysing the situation, Altunia arrived. He looked disturbed. " You must act now," he pleaded with Razia.

" You are as usual being impetuous. It is not so simple as you imagine."

" Simple! I don't say it is simple, but if you don't act now, we shall all face the same fate as Qutbuddin and his mother."

" The danger is there, but we must think hard. It is no use just rushing in. We have to weigh all the consequences of any action we may want to take, and then arrive at the best course to be adopted."

" All right, but then, our noble princess," said Altunia rather wearily, " let us think and plan and not waste time. Let's do something for God's sake or, God forbid, the whole empire may go to pieces, and all that the great Sultan laboured and struggled for these many years will lie in ruins. How truly Hanzala has put:

If leadership lies in the jaws of the lion
Go, and dare to grasp it from his jaws."

" Hanzala was a great thinker and he has, indeed, put it bravely, but you must not forget, Altunia, that to face a lion you must, first, be calm and careful. Haste will not do; nor should we allow our minds to become agitated. The bite of the lion is no peck of the chicken."

" That is right, Altunia," said Tajuddin, who, none the less, looked grim and serious.

" There are too many complications in a situation like this," added Razia, " and we must therefore sort them out first before deciding to strike."

" But can't we in the meantime do something to

restrain Shah Turkan?" implored Altunia. "She is a
maniac, a mad woman. She will destroy all of us."

"Don't worry, Altunia," said Razia confidently.
"The more she loses her balance the more she will expose
herself. Ultimately she will dig her own grave."

"But before she gets into it she may have dug our
graves. And that certainly worries me."

Razia did not reply immediately to Altunia's outburst.
For a moment she became pensive and said, "I see his
point, Tajuddin. I must admit that his apprehensions
are not all so ill founded." After a pause, she added,

"But why can't we question Shah Turkan? She is not the ruler. Let us petition the Nizamul Mulk to call the durbar so that we may request the Sultan to restrain his mother from committing further atrocities. What have you to say to it, Tajuddin?"

Tajuddin hesitated a little. How would they prove the charges? Shah Turkan had committed many wrongs, but under a legal cloak. Even Qutbuddin and her mother had been tried by a Tribunal. The atmosphere was, no doubt, hostile to her, but would that be enough to make the Sultan act against her? Tajuddin wondered. Nevertheless he agreed that in the prevailing circumstances it might be the best solution. It might arouse the Forty Amirs to the gravity of the situation and make them put a stop to the homicidal tendencies of the Sultan's mother, who, after all, continued in power at their pleasure.

On receiving Razia's petition, the Nizamul Mulk went to see her. He expressed his grave concern at the turn of events. He admitted that Shah Turkan had become a menace, but requested Razia to give him some time to set things right. A public exposure, he said, might make matters worse. It might so enrage Shah Turkan that she might indulge in worse crimes. He would, therefore, like to caution her firmly and sternly and to impress upon her the dire consequences of any unrestrained behaviour. Razia resisted the suggestion.

"Do you really believe that Shah Turkan will listen to you, Nizamul Mulk?"

"She may. After all, she cannot go on antagonising everybody."

"She has lost her balance. She is beyond reason," said Razia agitatedly.

"That may be so. But how will a public exposure help the situation?"

"The exposure must be followed by punishment," demanded Razia.

"But do you think the Sultan will ever agree to such a course?"

"You must make the Sultan agree," said Razia, with some firmness in her voice.

"I wish I could, but Shah Turkan's hold on him is greater than that of any of us," explained the Nizamul Mulk. "She has already alienated the Sultan's younger brother, Malik Ghiasuddin Muhammad, who has proved to be a much better Governor of Audh than we had expected. According to our information he has become much too ambitious and has decided to defy the Centre's authority. Then there are the revolts in Multan and Hansi, where Malik Izzuddin Ayaz and Malik Saifuddin Kuji have proclaimed respectively their severance with us. The Governor of Lahore, Malik Alauddin Jani, has also joined this conspiracy against the Sultanate. These are serious developments, pregnant with grim consequences for the empire. The Sultan will have to lead the forces in person against all these rebels if their pernicious designs are to be frustrated. After much persuasion he has agreed to do so. I do not want to upset him at such a time. Hence the caution, my good lady."

Razia thought over the request for a while. How could she be a party, in the remotest sense, to the disintegration of the empire? The empire must come first. The princess agreed, therefore, to wait for some time. Meanwhile, the Nizamul Mulk promised to prevail upon Shah Turkan to confine herself to the four corners of the palace and not to commit any further atrocities.

The Nizamul Mulk was, however, a wily, old fox. He thrived on intrigues in the court. He was as much responsible for allowing Shah Turkan to have her way as in playing one Amir against another. Therein lay the secret of his power! A public exposure of Shah Turkan would have been against his own interests. That was the reason why he got round Razia. As he grew in years, he had become more selfish and mean and less reliable and dependable. He had lost all sense of decency. Whatever honour or values he had once possessed, he had gradually discarded. All he wanted now was the retention of power and he was prepared to sacrifice anyone and anything at the altar of that power.

On returning from Razia, the Nizamul Mulk informed Shah Turkan that a plot was being hatched against her. But he cautioned her to lie low. A false step might let loose a storm against her; and in the absence of the Sultan from the capital this might lead to her ruination. He told her, therefore, not to be rash and reckless and jeopardise her own position.

But Shah Turkan had begun to lose faith in the Nizamul Mulk. Gradually she had come to realise that he would have no compunction in throwing her to the wolves if it suited his purpose. She, therefore, became suspicious of the old man and wondered whether he was not playing into Razia's hands. The time was also most opportune, she felt, with the Sultan busy fighting the insurrections in Badaun, Multan and Hansi, and the old fox free to try his hand at a new game to suit his purpose.

The more Shah Turkan pondered over the matter the more convinced she became that the Nizamul Mulk could not be trusted. With the passage of time she had come to hate him. Realising that he had used her for his own sake all this time, she decided to free herself from his hold and to act on her own. In this assessment of the Nizamul Mulk, Shah Turkan was not far wrong. Opportunism was his coin; appeasement, his method.

Anything that was good for the Nizamul Mulk was good for the empire; this had been almost a creed with Muhammad Junaidi and he lived up to it in all his dealings. The other Amirs danced to his tune for he was clever enough to adjust their interests to his own pattern of selfishness. But with all this, he did not want to do away with Shah Turkan; she still presented a counterpoise to Razia, which he was anxious not to disturb.

Distrustful of the Nizamul Mulk and afraid of the gathering storm around her, Shah Turkan proceeded to consolidate her position. After taking all aspects of the situation into account she decided that she must strike against Razia. There was no other alternative. Moreover, time had begun to run against her; she had to act as fast as she could. She brooded by day, kept awake by night. She thought of alternate schemes and finally concluded that it had to be something sharp and quick. Something which could work like lightning—strike and finish. For she knew that Razia was no Qutbuddin; no court would dare condemn her; no Amir could venture to harm her; no soldier would agree to kill her. And still Razia had to be killed if Shah Turkan was to survive in power and glory.

Silently and secretively she worked out the details of her diabolical plot. On her own she planned everything. Apart from her trusted men, none had the slightest inkling of the working of her mind. She was neither daunted by the enormity of the crime she planned nor shaken by the terrible risk involved in it. Only when in the preparations she encountered some hitch, here and there, she became frustrated and burnt with impatience; but otherwise she was in the grip of a fierce spirit of revenge. As the preparations were completed, her murderous instinct sharpened as never before.

Thereafter she did not want a moment to be lost. The execution of the plot became an obsession with her, the be-all and end-all of her existence. A rogue at heart, she enjoyed her vices more than any virtue she possessed.

6

THE DISCOVERY AT NIGHT

THOUGH Razia was perturbed about the state of affairs in the empire—both inside the palace and outside in the provinces—she hardly ever thought of her own safety. Adored by all sections of the people, even those Amirs who were opposed to her succession had a certain affection for her. In their eyes Razia was set apart from other persons. True, because of their deep-rooted prejudice —or maybe apprehensions—she was not acceptable to them as a ruler. But none of them could ever think of doing her harm. Disarmingly good to all, she had never caused an affront to anyone and hence none could have any malice towards her. Moreover, her devotion to the empire compelled universal admiration.

During the reign of Iltutmish, she had served on several occasions as his deputy and her talents were widely recognised. The late Sultan had even included her name in the *tanka* or the silver coin, which he was the first to introduce in India. From the early days of her youth the princess had plunged into the service of the empire and every Amir was conscious of the single-minded devotion and sense of dedication with which she had worked. Except for the throne there was nothing which, if Razia asked for, would not have been given by them.

However, because of the activities of Shah Turkan, Altunia apprehended danger. So long as the pernicious atmosphere prevailed at the court, he refused to be complacent. Repeatedly he warned Razia and Tajuddin about a possible conspiracy. But Razia felt that he was being unduly suspicious. After all, Shah Turkan could not be so blind to the terrible repercussions of any design against the princess of the realm; with all her devilry she could not get away with it.

" I know you are a brave lady," Altunia told Razia one day, " but bravery is no match for trickery and deceit."

" I agree. But is it so easy for anyone to kill me, Altunia? Don't you realise that it would shake the whole structure of the empire?"

" May be, but do you think Shah Turkan cares for the empire?"

" She cares for herself, doesn't she? What would be her own fate if she kills me? Do you think she would be able to survive it?"

" That woman is the devil incarnate. She is capable of anything."

" What do you want me to do then? Plot against Shah Turkan?"

" No, but we must at least prepare ourselves to foil any plot that she might be hatching against you."

" In other words you want me to organise against the Sultan, but that, as I have repeatedly told you, will not be proper."

" Proper or not, it must be done. Do you realise what would be our fate if anything ever happens to you? It would be the end of all of us and of the whole empire as well."

After a pause, Altunia added, rather impulsively, " And have you ever thought of my feelings? Oh! I know you don't care, but for me life without you has no meaning. This is the truth, Razia, and I must tell you that even though it may embarrass you."

" Why should it embarrass me, Altunia. On the contrary, I am touched by your sentiment. I know how much you love me. I am also, believe me, extremely fond of you. You have a strange influence over me. I have never experienced such emotions before. I feel we are destined to be together. And still this is not the time to think of ourselves. We must not allow such emotions to get the better of us."

" But why, Razia? That is not being human. We are both young; we belong to the same race; we have a right to love."

" Yes, we have," replied Razia thoughtfully. " But there are moments when one should be able to rise above all personal considerations. Do you think I don't feel as strongly as you do? Or that I have no emotions and feelings? But we are not free to do what we like with ourselves. No, Altunia, we are committed to the welfare of our people. Their interests must come before our own."

" But why should there be any conflict between our personal happiness and the interests of the people?" asked Altunia.

" Ordinarily there should be none. But these are difficult times and the situation is becoming more and more grave day by day. You yourself have been warning me. Unless I concentrate on the affairs of the empire, I shall be betraying the trust reposed in me by my father."

" I don't understand you, Razia. You act strangely. Why are you bent upon curbing all emotions? What is life without emotions? You are not only being cruel to me but also to yourself."

" Perhaps you are right, Altunia. But, then, this

seems to be the path I must tread for the present. I have no alternative."

Altunia realised that Razia could not be dissuaded. She had a mind of her own. As a man, proud and self-assured, he found it difficult to understand her. She was a woman and still so different from other women. In fact, Razia had had little contact with other women. Even during the reign of Iltutmish, she had rarely mixed with the inmates of the harem and had been preoccupied with the affairs of the state. Consequently she was surrounded by men and grew up untutored in the ways of women. This inculcated in her, no doubt, a feeling of equality with men but in the process she lost something —that peculiar submissiveness of a woman which could be equally effective against men.

Altunia loved Razia deeply; but he could not penetrate the armour of her aloofness. Often he tried to make her lose herself in the ecstasies of an intimate, human relationship; but he could not succeed. There was something inexplicable about her, which held her back. Whether it was a " psychological block " or complete absorption in the affairs of the empire, or whether it was her orthodox upbringing or the fear of consequences, whatever it be, Razia would not let her emotions have the better of her. No sooner was she drawn into the whirlpool of romance than she managed to get out of it. It seemed as if she had some peculiar dread of the outcome.

Meanwhile Shah Turkan, frightened by what lay in store for her as a result of her own evil deeds, decided upon striking against Razia, the root—according to her— of all her trouble. She consulted some of her confidants in her efforts to carry out her sinister plot. She knew of Razia's extreme fondness for horse-riding. Right from her childhood, the princess rode a horse as skilfully as she rode an elephant. It was her routine, ever since the days of her father, to go to the royal stables each morning and choose the swiftest horse, then, while riding it, to make it jump over a high, strongly built-up fence, at a particular spot. The stables used to be in charge of a black Abyssynian slave—Jamaluddin Yaqut. He had looked after it as a boy until he rose to be the lord of the stables. Tall and straight, he had a head almost like a Greek god's; his countenance was pale, calm and expressive; his mouth full of loveliness, his hair dark and curly and his skin was fine, clear and transparent. His manner was pleasing; his voice had a soft, melodious ring. Iltutmish liked him immensely; he became almost a part of the royal family. He and Razia had known each other since their childhood; in fact they grew up together. As the years passed, they became good friends; during Razia's morning rides, Yaqut used to be her constant companion all through the years.

So Shah Turkan, in accordance with the outlines of her diabolical plot, arranged to have the ground, near the built-up fence, where Razia galloped the horse every morning, dug deep, and then the ground to be so covered as not to be noticeable at all. Since Razia would not be aware of it, the horse, while galloping, would land on the spot—the fall would be instantaneously fatal to both horse and rider. The incident could easily be explained away as an accident; before enquiries could be made, and by taking immediate advantage of the general commotion, which would necessarily follow the "accident", the ground could be quickly filled in. That, in short, was the plot.

Apart from some of her most trusted men, Shah Turkan did not take anyone else into confidence. She also remained indoors, leading a quiet life. The Nizamul Mulk was happy. He got the impression that his advice had at last worked. One day he went to Razia and boasted of his achievement. The princess admitted that by his shrewd handling of the situation the Nizamul Mulk had succeeded in bringing about the desired change in Shah Turkan.

Razia teased Altunia about his undue anxiety and asked him to cheer up now that his fears had proved baseless. Tajuddin agreed that the atmosphere in the palace had changed for the better. There was much less terror in the air, and people moved about more freely. Sceptical as ever, Altunia wondered whether it was the proverbial lull before the storm. But Razia implored him not to be such a cynic.

Shah Turkan, meanwhile, went ahead with her sinister preparations. The night before the appointed morning, her chosen servants went to the spot and in the darkest hours of the night began digging the ground. Just then Yaqut, on suddenly recollecting that he had forgotten to tie one of the most favourite of Razia's horses, rushed to the stables. On his way he heard some noise. Going nearer he saw some strange men at work. Not understanding what it was all about, yet suspicious of their activities in the middle of the night, he crept nearer and hid there to see what was going on. At once he realised that it was the same spot where Razia galloped her horse each morning. After the digging was over, the men at work put a thin covering on the ground, and levelled it so perfectly that nothing could be noticed. Then they looked around to make sure that they had not been seen and tiptoed out from there, soon disappearing into the darkness of the night.

At first Yaqut was somewhat intrigued and could not fathom the implications of their action but then he realised the gravity of what he had seen and, at once, rushed to Razia's bed-chamber. It was past midnight

and the princess was fast asleep. Parveen dared not wake
her up. Yaqut pleaded urgency but the maid-in-waiting
was firm. Finally he brushed her aside and ran into the
bed-chamber. In the commotion Razia woke up.

" Please pardon me, my princess, but I had to take this
liberty," Yaqut said with the utmost submission.

Astonished at the sudden intrusion, Razia got out of
bed with a start and asked Yaqut as to what was the
matter.

" I need privacy," he implored.

" From my maid-in-waiting," demanded Razia sternly,
" and at this hour! Whatever is the matter can it not
wait till morning?"

" No, my noble lady! I must speak to you at once
and alone. It is very urgent. We cannot afford to lose
time."

The princess sensed the alarm in Yaqut's tone and
asked Parveen to withdraw. Then Yaqut narrated all
that he had seen. Razia saw the hand of Shah Turkan
in the whole affair. She asked him to wake up Altunia
and Tajuddin and bring them to her bed-chamber.
Yaqut left, worried and concerned.

Stunned and dazed, Razia sat up. She could not
believe her ears. True, she had always known Shah
Turkan to be cruel, callous and unscrupulous but that
she—the wife of her own father, who had shared his life
with her for so many years—could stoop so low was
beyond the princess's wildest imagination.

7

THE DAWN OF ACCESSION

ALL through the night, until the break of dawn, the four of them—Razia, Altunia, Tajuddin and Yaqut—remained closeted together. They deliberated anxiously, they argued animatedly. Their main problem was: how to trap Shah Turkan? Her plot had not only to be foiled; it had to be effectively exposed. But that was no easy task for she had powerful friends among the Amirs to protect her. Every precaution had therefore to be taken to establish her personal role in the crime and to prove her direct involvement in its commission. After anxious consideration, a scheme was formulated; it was as perfect as the combined wisdom of the four could make it.

As a first step, a few selected groups were taken into confidence. These included some of the leading Amirs, a few among the bodyguards and some trusted officers of the Imperial Army. That done, some among the *ulema* were summoned to the palace and informed vaguely of the plot. They were asked to send word to the imams in the mosques, where the faithful were to assemble for their morning prayers. The result was that from mouth to mouth the version changed; in no time the whole city was agog with wild rumours. Thousands of people rushed to the riding ground, and waited anxiously, expecting to witness an exciting situation.

At the appointed time Razia arrived, clad in a red garment customary for the aggrieved. She rode her horse, and went a little distance away from the fence. Suddenly she dug her spurs into the horse. He came near the fence and leaped forward at almost a full gallop. The princess gave the animal his head, but just as she was leading him into the jump she held him back with full force and asked the Nizamul Mulk to examine the spot where the horse was to land. In a moment the ground collapsed, making a big hole. The unfolding of the plot was so dramatic that the assembled gathering gasped. Razia asked the Nizamul Mulk to send for Shah Turkan. He hesitated at first, but, sensing the mood of the people, obeyed. Shah Turkan realised that all was lost; she became nervous and refused to come out. The whole exposure had been so sudden and unexpected that she could not muster courage to face the consequences. Moreover, the circumstantial evidence against her was so overwhelming that a flat denial would have only confirmed her guilt.

Razia asked the Nizamul Mulk whether he was aware of what was happening at the palace?· What sort of Prime Minister was he? She then produced the servants who had dug the ground, and, who, by clever manœuvring on the part of Altunia and Tajuddin, had been picked up just as they were about to leave the site after completing the preparations for their murderous act. Nervous and pale and shivering with fright, they narrated how Shah Turkan had engaged them to kill Razia.

The people were mad with anger; the soldiers reacted violently; the bodyguards demanded the head of Shah Turkan. The Nizamul Mulk tried to pacify them, but such was their fury that they shouted him down. Sensing danger to his own life, he took to his heels. Some of the soldiers chased him; but Razia stopped them. Unless it was proved that he had a hand in the crime, no harm should come to him, she said.

" But what about Shah Turkan? Where is she? We are not going to leave her alone?" the people shouted.

The demand for her seizure became insistent. The princess feared that the crowd might get out of control. She therefore despatched Altunia with a contingent of soldiers to bring Shah Turkan to the riding ground. She was, however, to be treated with the courtesy and respect befitting the wife of the late Sultan.

The suspense only added to the excitement. It was clear that the new Sultan's rule had not only created chaos

and disorder but also much resentment among the people. They hated Shah Turkan for her cruelties, her crass selfishness and her complete disregard of the most elementary human values. With the passage of time she had so covered herself with the heap of her own bad deeds that everyone, high and low, detested her.

As Shah Turkan was being brought to the riding ground by Altunia and the soldiers who had accompanied him, the Sultan arrived at the head of his huge forces, after having successfully suppressed the rebellions in different provinces. Accompanying him were many leading Amirs such as Bahaul Mulk Hussain, Karimuddin Zahid, Ziaul Mulk Junaidi, Rashiduddin Malkani, Nizamuddin Sharkani and Amir Fakhruddin.

Seeing the crowd and the excitement, the Sultan looked for the Nizamul Mulk, but in vain, and then turned to Razia and asked her what was the matter.

Seizing the opportunity, the princess narrated, graphically and dramatically, all that had happened. She could not have been more eloquent and convincing. As the words fell from her mouth, she captured the hearts of the Amirs and the soldiers. Instinctively their sympathies went out to her. They joined the people gathered there in demanding the head of Shah Turkan.

The Sultan was flabbergasted. He resisted the demand and in a fit of anger aeclared that, instead of his mother, he would put Razia to death. He accused her of having plotted against him while he had been away.

The declaration added fuel to the fire; it inflamed the wrath of the people. They became rebellious and shouted for the head of the Sultan. Even the Amirs, loyal to the Sultan, lost courage; they detached themselves from him and went over to the other side. Their action was a climax to the rebellion. One battalion

after another revolted against the Sultan and went over
to the side of Razia.

On the edge of collapse, the Sultan gave up, and ran
hither and thither. But he was finally caught; so was
his mother, Shah Turkan, whom the mob and the infu-
riated soldiers were about to lynch. In the commotion
a voice was heard; it was the voice of the saint—Malik
Kazimuddin Zahid. He pleaded for patience and asked
the people not to take the law into their own hands.

" But where is the law?" demanded the people.

" You are right," said the saint. " There is no law.
Hence our first duty is to establish the rule of law. That
is why I demand, in the name of the Amirs, the soldiers
and the people, the deposition of Sultan Ruknuddin and
the installation in his place of our noble lady, Sultan
Razia, the choice of our late Sultan and the beloved of
our people, as our new ruler."

There was an instant outburst of approval from the
assembled crowd. The soldiers supported it exuberant-
ly; the bodyguards hailed the choice. Even those Amirs
who did not like the succession because of their old prejudice against Razia dared not oppose it. The die had
been cast. Amidst thunderous applause and rejoicing,
Razia was proclaimed the new Sultan.

Thanking the Amirs, the soldiers and the people for
the trust that they had reposed in her, she declared:
" I promise you before God that I shall try to prove
worthy of your trust. And because I am born a woman,
I here and now enter into a solemn agreement with my
Amirs, my soldiers and my people that I shall sit on this
great throne of our ancestors only if I prove to be better
than men, and that, if I fail to carry out this solemn
undertaking, you will be free to cut off my head and give
the throne to whomsoever you judge to be worthy of
that honour. And as our Prophet used to say in a

moment of victory, so do I pray: ' O Allah! I seek Thy
refuge from misleading others and from being misled by
others; from betraying others into error and from being
betrayed by others into error; from doing wrong to
others and from being wronged by others; from drawing
others into ignorance and from being drawn by others
into ignorance; from any harshness that I may show to
others and from any harshness that others may show to
me. And from any sin that thou, Lord, mayst not
forgive!' "

Then she ordered the arrest of the deposed Sultan
Ruknuddin and his mother Shah Turkan. The new
ruler, however, promised that they would be tried according to the laws of Islam and, only if found guilty,
punished.

They were subsequently tried and found guilty and
were executed on November 9, 1236. Their rule had
lasted a little more than six months.

8

A BREATH OF FRESH AIR

Razia's accession to the throne came as a breath of fresh air to the entire Sultanate. She was the picture of calm and sweet majesty, of infinite tenderness for all and compassion for the poor. Devoting herself wholeheartedly to the welfare of the state, she embarked on many a new measure to alleviate the hunger and suffering of her subjects. First, she brought order, where chaos had prevailed; secondly, she geared up the administrative machinery; and, finally, she introduced many reforms to improve the social and economic lot of the people. Her heart pulsated for every section, high and low; in their welfare she saw the real strength of the Sultanate.

Anxious to march forward, she sought the co-operation of all in the new tasks that awaited her. She was particularly anxious to enlist the support of the Forty Amirs, assuring them that they should entertain no fears because of their past prejudice against her. As their Queen, Razia promised every Amir that she would be fair and just to all, for she believed that however powerful might be the lures of favouritism, these should vanish when a person ascended the throne.

As a gesture of good will, she continued Muhammad Junaidi—despite his murky past—as the Nizamul Mulk. Similarly she restored to their high positions Maliks Jani,

Kuji and Ayaz. True, she leaned heavily on her trusted friends, especially Tajuddin and Altunia, who enjoyed her complete trust and were, consequently, given the most significant posts, but in the general selection of office-holders she gave due recognition to merit, with the result that during her reign some of the talented young Turks were inducted into responsible positions for the first time.

She tried to win over the Forty Amirs; they were treated with respect and shown high consideration. The Queen never failed to consult them on matters of policy; on all other important measures, too, they were taken into her confidence. But Razia could not be a tool in their hands: she had a mind of her own; she possessed fresh ideas; she was inspired by a new approach. Being dynamic, she was eager to venture into pastures new; being devoted to the cause of the Sultanate, she was determined to strengthen the whole pattern of its administration. This was no easy task, for she knew that most of the Amirs were apprehensive of any radical change; but she pursued her course of action with vigour and energy. Tactfully she handled each situation as it arose; but she rarely faltered or failed in what she wanted to do. Soon the most powerful of the Amirs became suspicious of her reforms and saw in them a danger to their own position. Moreover, they did not like her frequent appearances in public and the manner in which she encouraged people to approach her for the redress of their grievances. They insisted that being a woman she should maintain a distance.

" In your illustrious father's time, Your Majesty, you never appeared so openly before the public. A thin veil covered your noble face," the Nizamul Mulk reminded the Queen one day.

"But in my father's time I was not the ruler," replied Razia. "I cannot afford to keep any distance now between myself and my subjects. I must make them feel that I am their protector. I cannot close my doors on them. How does the question of my sex arise here? When I am with my people I am not a woman: I am their custodian and guardian."

"True! True! Your Majesty, but you are a woman and when they see you so often they become more conscious of that fact."

"How perverted you have become, Nizamul Mulk! Do you feel like that when you talk to me?" asked Razia.

Shocked at the remark, the Nizamul Mulk exclaimed, "How can you talk like this, my noble lady! You are just like my daughter."

"So am I to my people. I am like a mother to them. My being young should make no difference. They are pure in thought and noble in their behaviour. When I look into their eyes, I see their agonies and sufferings. And when they come to me they don't come to a woman but they come to the fountain of justice to quench their thirst."

"I appreciate your noble attitude, Your Majesty. But tongues wag and we have to be careful," observed the Nizamul Mulk.

"I know the tongues that wag. I expect you to silence them," commanded the Queen. "You must tell the Amirs that my behaviour is a part of my faith."

"They are only trying to be helpful, Your Majesty," pleaded the Nizamul Mulk.

"I see," said Razia in a tone of sarcasm. "That is why they have not yet got over their prejudice against my being a woman. I would like you to tell them that I am proud of the fact that I am a woman! Do you know that there is more majesty in a woman's heart than dwells in the crowns of a hundred kings? God created us to temper men; you would have been brutes without us."

"I am all for women, Your Majesty. But women are so gentle and weak; they need to be protected," submitted the Nizamul Mulk.

"Protected against whom? Against your fellow men?

You want us to wear a veil—purdah—but why should you subject us to such humiliation when the sin does not lie in us but in the eyes of men? Instead of our faces, your eyes and your minds should be veiled," remarked Razia.

" That is the teaching of our religion, Your Majesty " said the Nizamul Mulk.

" Who says so? It is men like you who have corrupted our religion and the teachings of our Prophet. Can you show me a single line in the Quran, which supports this? The Prophet lifted women out of the slough of despair and gave them a new status! His wife, Aisha, commanded forces; his beloved daughter, Fatima, took an active part in the politics of Arabia; his granddaughter, Sakina, fought like a brave woman, sword in hand, on the battle-field of Karbala. Do not talk to me of the teachings of our religion. It is you men, who, in order to gratify your possessive instinct and to maintain your superiority over us, have twisted and corrupted these teachings to suit your own purposes."

" I am sorry, Your Majesty," submitted the Nizamul Mulk, once again. " I find I have upset you."

" I am not upset. In fact I am grateful to you for having given me an opportunity to unburden myself. I have been wanting to do so for some time. I feel much relieved."

" May I take your leave now, Your Majesty?" asked the Nizamul Mulk with great humility.

" Yes, you may go; but there is one thing which I would like you to do. Please get inscribed on my coins the expression: *Umdatul Niswan* or " Illustrious among women ". It will be a constant reminder to the Amirs to adjust their mental outlook to the changed situation. And, believe me, they will, in the long run, feel the happier for it."

Just as the Nizamul Mulk left, Altunia arrived.
" Here comes another man!" exclaimed Razia, greet-
ing him. The young Amir was taken aback; he could
not understand Razia's strange behaviour.
" What is the matter, Razia?" asked Altunia.
" Are you also prejudiced against me because I am a
woman?"
" How can I be? I love you!"
" Of course, you do. That is why you cannot be prejudiced. In fact you are happy that I am a woman. I
suppose all men like women, but only when they are in
love with them; otherwise they have no use for them."
" Why are you talking like this? Has anything
happened?"
" Nothing, my dear Altunia. I am just wondering
about human relationships! You see, I am happy
because I am a woman, but perhaps I would be still
happier if there were no men around to trouble women.
They demand everything from us, but what do they give
us in return? Love, they say. Selfish creatures! They
do not know the meaning of the word."
" Have I done anything to offend you, Razia? Why
are you talking to me like this?"
" I am sorry, Altunia, it is not you but men in general
that I am thinking of. You have been a good friend.
You have always stood by me; my life would be empty
without you. I love you. But ever since I became the
Queen, I am becoming more and more disturbed about
the behaviour of my Amirs towards me. Basically they
are so egoistical, self-centred, jealous and possessive.
They find it difficult to get adjusted to the present situation, where they are required to bow to my wishes. Not
that I order them about; but they resent the very relationship. It seems to go against their grain. I do not know
how to deal with them."

"I think you are positively angry with me! Somebody has poisoned you against me," said Altunia, rather dejectedly.

"That is not true, Altunia. No one can succeed in doing it. I have known you since my childhood; we have been such wonderful friends. I wish my other Amirs were as good and understanding as you have been."

"Has anything gone wrong, Razia."

"No! No!" replied Razia, a bit exasperated. "I am only thinking about the men who surround me all the time and still remain such an enigma. Every time I try to solve this riddle that is man, it eludes me."

"I think you are tired. You'd better retire and rest," implored Altunia, who did not want to argue with Razia on a subject over which she felt so bitter and angry because of the machinations of her jealous Amirs.

9

AN EFFORT AT INTEGRATION

THOUGH Razia was thus embittered by the Amirs' cussed-
ness and lack of understanding, she was not deterred
from carrying out many of the reforms on which she had
set her heart.   Some of these were no doubt radical, such
as decentralisation of power and lavish expenditure
on building roads, planting trees and digging wells,
which helped to create a tremendous reservoir of goodwill for the Queen among the lower ranks of officers and
ordinary folks.   But the Amirs saw a twofold danger in
these measures: first, curtailment of their authority, and,
secondly, diversion of monies from their pockets to public works.   They had reconciled themselves to the
Queen's public appearances, her moving about frequent-
ly among the citizens of Delhi, her holding meetings with
the poets whose work she enjoyed, her discourses with
the learned and her supervision of the day-to-day work
of the officers; but they resented the reforms which hit
them directly and undermined their position.

One day Razia suggested to the Amirs the abolition
of the *Jazziah* or the poll-tax on the non-Muslims
(*Zimmis*, as they were called in Islam), imposed on
religious grounds.   The Amirs vehemently opposed the
step.   Their case was forcefully argued by a young member of the clan who had suddenly begun to make his

mark: Ghiasuddin Balban, a distant relative of Razia.
He was rather ugly looking because of his pockmarked
face, but he was extremely able and intelligent. He had
been purchased as a slave by Iltutmish. The Sultan, it
was said, had first refused to buy him because of his
ugliness and short stature.

"Why have you bought these others?" Balban had
asked.

"For my sake," Iltutmish had replied.

"Then buy me, O Master of the world, for the sake
of God."

And the Sultan had obliged.

Beginning his life as a *bhishti* or water-carrier, Balban rose, with the passage of time, to the office of chief huntsman. He boasted of his descent from the Khakhans of Albari, the ancestors of Iltutmish, and was fanatically devoted to his tribal cause. Exceedingly ambitious, he did not want that Razia should take any step that might weaken the authority of the tribe and deprive the treasury of a tried and profitable source of revenue.

" But how does the abolition of the tax weaken our authority?" the Queen demanded of Balban.

" It does, Your Majesty. The tax is a reminder to our Hindu subjects that we are their rulers," said Balban.

" I am not impressed; such humiliation is no reminder; it is only a provocation to them," pointed out Razia. " It will not inspire any loyalty in them to the throne. On the contrary, it will cause more and more resentment. After all, I have also many Muslim subjects. Should they also not be reminded that I am their ruler?"

" But your Muslim subjects, Your Majesty, are obliged to take up arms for you; the Hindu subjects are exempt from such an obligation. That is why they pay the tax. In return they are assured of the protection of life and property," explained Balban.

" Supposing some of my Hindu subjects desire to take up arms for me, can they?" asked Razia.

" No, because we cannot trust them," replied Balban.

" Why—because they are not Muslims and so we must force this humiliation on them?"

" It is also an invitation to them, Your Majesty, to join the fold of Islam," said Balban.

" This is no way of spreading Islam! Have you forgotten what the Quran enjoins on us: ' There shall be no compulsion in religion '?"

" There is no compulsion in this, Your Majesty," said

Balban. "If the Hindus do not want to be converted, they may continue to be Hindus; they just have to pay the tax."

"Do you know the history of this tax?" asked Razia. "It was imposed in the early period of Islam on non-believers because most of the wars were then fought on grounds of our particular faith, and such persons as did not subscribe to that faith could not be expected to fight. The believers, on the other hand, were obliged to do military service."

"That was the origin of this tax; but since then its connotation has changed considerably and the *ulema* have upheld it," argued Balban.

"To suit either their whims or the caprices of their rulers," retorted Razia. "Oh, don't talk to me about the *ulema*. There are, no doubt, some notable exceptions; but many of them are more interested in politics than in religion. That has been our bane. Why? What did Najmuddin Sughara, whom my father appointed as Shakh-ul Islam, or leader of Islam, do? He tried some of the dirtiest tricks with that really great saint, Shaikh Jalaluddin Tabrizi. He even charged him with having committed adultery with Gauhar, a nautch-girl of Delhi, so that he could replace him. That is the depth to which some of them could stoop."

"Still I submit, Your Majesty, that the distinction between believers and non-believers in Islam is clear cut. The preference is well established and we must honour it," said Balban.

"Religion cannot be understood in parts; it must be taken as a whole. Its spirit is more important than its texts," replied Razia. "Do you know that the Prophet once warned, ' Beware! On the day of judgment I shall myself be the complainant against him who wrongs a *Zimmi* or lays on him a responsibility greater than he can bear or deprives him of anything that belongs to him '."

" I am enlightened, Your Majesty, but in this land we are surrounded by Hindus. That is why we have to be careful."

" The danger is not so much from my Hindu subjects as from our own religious bigots, who have made a mockery of Islam," observed the Queen. She added, " I am surprised, Balban, that a man of your learning and ability should have such narrow views on a tax like the *Jazziah*. Do you think its imposition will ever help us to spread Islam among the people here? Do you think it will ever make them accept us as their rulers? I am afraid we are not really serving the cause of Islam, or for that matter even of our empire!"

" The tax is not new; it has been imposed ever since the Muslims came to India. Can't you see, Your Majesty, how it has helped to spread Islam among the Hindus, how many of them have been converted to our faith?" urged Balban with great feeling.

" Maybe, many Hindus embraced Islam out of fear," agreed Razia. " But many more were converted by our saints and sufis; the purity and simplicity of their lives and the broad humanism of their message had a great effect on the good and simple people of India. They flocked to these saints and were comforted by their words."

" They were, no doubt, great spiritual leaders, but don't you think that their approach was a departure from the puritanism of Islam?" asked Balban.

" How can you say that, Balban?" exclaimed the Queen. " Puritanism lies in love—not in compulsion." She added, " Don't you know how thousands of Hindus came, of their own free will, to Shaikh Ali bin Usman al-Hujwairi, also known as Data Ganj Baksh, whose tomb at Lahore is one of the most popular shrines in our Sultanate?   He was the founder of Sufism in India.   And what about Khwaja Moinuddin Chishti, the great saint of Ajmer, to whom people rushed from far and near as do deer to a waterfall?   He left this world for his eternal abode only a few years ago but such has been the impact

of his teachings that hundreds of devotees gather round
his tomb every day, deriving solace and comfort, and find-
ing new strength to face the problems of life. By love and
dedication these men of God brought the Hindus to a
better understanding of Islam, with the result that even
those who did not become Muslims developed respect for
our religion. That is the way to conduct ourselves; that
is how the work of Allah should be carried out: not by
force—for force destroys the human heart."

"But we are not saints, Your Majesty. We have to
rule, and one cannot rule without resort to force."

"True, but what is gained by the sword shall perish
by the sword; on the contrary, what love gives is indes-
tructible. I want all my subjects to have a feeling of
love for the throne so that they may protect it with their
lives. That is why I want to abolish this tax and make
the Hindus a part of our empire."

"That is not possible, Your Majesty," submitted Balban. "Please don't misunderstand me, but the Hindus
cannot become a part of our empire. They will never
be reconciled to our rule."

"You are wrong, Balban," replied Razia. "The fault
lies with us, not with them. Our whole approach
towards them is unsympathetic. We do not mix with
them; we don't share in their joys and sorrows; we are a
race apart from them, and we take pride in maintaining
this separation. We may be the rulers and they the
ruled; but why do we want to inculcate fear in them?
Why can't we try and bring them nearer to us?"

"But we are so different from them, Your Majesty.
We are Turks, they are Indians; we are Muslims, they
are Hindus. How can the two become one; that is
against human nature."

"I wish you men really knew something of human
nature. If you did, then we wouldn't have had all this

trouble in the world," remarked Razia, reacting rather bitterly.

Balban was not, however, alone in holding such views. The more powerful of the Amirs were even more reactionary. Razia was conscious of the disaffection that the abolition would cause among them, but she believed the move would have a tremendous effect on her Hindu subjects, inculcating in them a better sense of loyalty towards the throne. Hence she went ahead with her plan.

Right at that time, Razia received the sad news of the death of Malik Saifuddin Aibak, who was in charge of the strong fortress of Ranthambhor, where, since the time of Iltutmish, the Chauhans had valiantly defied the might of the imperial forces. Eventually they had been subdued but they had never left either the fortress or the town in peace. In the beginning the commander had managed to hold the fortress but no sooner did the Chauhans learn of his death than they mobilised their forces, and once again marched on the fortress, encircling the imperial troops.

In the wake of the abolition of the tax, such defiance by the Chauhans proved hardly helpful to Razia. Not only Balban but also Ayaz and the Nizamul Mulk struck a note of warning, demanding sterner action against the Hindus. Razia urged them not to become panicky and despatched immediately Malik Qutbuddin Hussain, one of her most trusted lieutenants, to Ranthambhor.

On assuming the command, the Malik was able to break through the encirclement and relieve the fortress, rescuing the troops. On receipt of the glad tidings, Razia instructed the Malik to withdraw the imperial forces, abandon the fortress and return to Delhi.

The Amirs were horrified at this action. How could a victorious army behave in this manner? It would only

encourage the Hindus to foment more trouble everywhere. The Nizamul Mulk expressed grave concern; he
told the Queen that her policy would destroy the
Sultanate.

" But don't you realise it is impossible to hold the
fortress in the face of such defiance by the Chauhans?
My father tried it for years, and what happened?" asked
Razia.

" What happened?" asked the Nizamul Mulk, rather
agitatedly and added, " He subjugated them."

" For how long? Didn't they rise again and again?
What is the use of a victory which eludes us every time
we win it? No, Nizamul Mulk, that is not my way of
governing the people; I do want to conquer them but in
a more civilised manner."

" And do you really believe, Your Majesty, that sur-
rendering to them like this is more civilised?" asked the
Nizamul Mulk.

" What did my grandfather, Qutbuddin Aibak, do?
Did he not allow the Rajput princes to rule over Delhi,
Ajmer and Gwalior, even after these places had been
conquered by him?"

" Those were different days; it was the time of the
beginning of our dynasty."

" I don't agree. I think it is the only way of winning
over the Hindus, who are so much more numerous than
we are. The strength of my empire does not depend
on one Ranthambhor; it depends on the sense of peace
and security that I am able to give to my people. The
Hindu rajas, who are all disunited, would willingly surrender to our superior arms if they knew that we would
treat them with honour and respect. You cannot humi-
liate a people and expect them to be loyal to you."

" I am afraid your approach would disrupt the empire;
it would embolden the Hindus to rise and rebel against

us; it would generate a seditious movement against the Sultanate," submitted Balban who had accompanied the Nizamul Mulk.

"You are shortsighted and are being unnecessarily afraid. It is only by liberalism in our outlook that we can secure our empire. When Jerusalem surrendered to Umar, the second Caliph of Islam, he guaranteed to the *Zimmis* security of life and property, protection to their crosses and churches and maintenance of their honour and dignity. When he was dying at the assassin's hands, he exclaimed, ' To him who will be Caliph after me, I command my wish and testament: The *Zimmis* are protected of Allah and the Prophet. Respect the covenants made with them and when necessary even fight for their interests.' That was the approach of a man of vision, Balban."

But neither Balban nor the Nizamul Mulk nor their compatriots in the Turkish hierarchy believed in such an approach. Aggressive by temperament and motivated by avarice, greed and the lust for power, they were becoming alarmed at what they considered the idiosyncrasies of a Queen who was determined to change every norm of the Sultanate and to remould it according to the dictates of her heart.

Often, while by herself, she recited, softly and for her own ears, the following verses of Saadi:

Take care of the poor and the needy
And remember that the ruler owes his crown to the
people.
The people are the roots and the ruler is the tree,
And the tree depends on the roots
Do not offend the people's feelings.
If you do, you uproot yourself.

10

REVOLTS SUPPRESSED

As Razia grew more assertive and firm, the Amirs became more restive. They decided to challenge her authority for they were convinced, that, unless they acted soon, whatever power remained with them would also be lost. The foxy Nizamul Mulk, on whom the Queen continued to rely because of his long association with the royal family, again took the leading part in secretly organising the revolt against her. He was helped by the Maliks Jani and Kuji and by that powerful general, Izzuddin Ayaz. All the four wrote confidential letters to the provincial governors, giving false and gruesome details of Razia's rule and instigating them to rise against her. They were assured by the four that they were engaged in similar preparations against the Queen in Delhi, the capital.

One of the provincial governors betrayed the contents of the letter to Altunia, who warned Razia in time about the plot. The combination looked so powerful that the Queen became perturbed. She instructed Altunia to gather round him all the reliable Amirs and officers and to keep them ready for all possible eventualities; but she knew that her side was far too weak. She, therefore, summoned to Delhi one of her most trusted lieutenants: Malik Izzuddin Hansi, the governor of Audh. He came with all his forces. However, as he was crossing the Ganga, the hostile Amirs sent their men to fight him. After a bitter encounter, he was seized. Already an ailing man, the shock of his defeat and humiliation killed him.

To Razia, his death came as a severe blow; it emboldened the Nizamul Mulk and the other Amirs to rise at once against her. However, as they were preparing to capture her, she organised her officers and men, placed them on the bank of the river Jamuna, and pitched her own tent there, within the sight of everyone in Delhi. This was, indeed, a clever move because the hostile Amirs knew how popular the Queen was with the people. They, therefore, hesitated before taking military action. But, while talks were going on among them as to how she was to be captured, Razia was successful in sowing the seeds of dissension among the rebellious Amirs.

One night she asked Altunia to spread the rumour in the enemy's camp, through her trusted spies, that the Nizamul Mulk was making overtures to the Queen with the help of Maliks Kochi and Jani. Since the Amirs distrusted one another, the rumour caused immediate consternation among the rival groups; it especially alarmed Maliks Salari and Ayaz, both of whom had always suspected the wily Nizamul Mulk.

Taking advantage of the situation, Altunia, who happened to be on friendly terms in the past with Ayaz, arranged a secret meeting between Salari and Ayaz and the Queen. At the same time the news of their secret compact was spread in time to the Nizamul Mulk and his group and they became apprehensive.

The plan worked so well that the Queen, with the help of Salari and Ayaz, seized Jani and Kochi; their capture completely demoralised their side. The Nizamul Mulk took fright and fled; Razia's men pursued him but he

disappeared into the Simur Hills, where he soon died—
a lone fugitive.

The successful suppression of the revolt did tremendous good to Razia. It not only re-established her
supremacy but strengthened her position. As a mark of
appreciation, she awarded the most important governorship, that of Lahore, to Ayaz, and put Altunia in charge
of the powerful province of Bhatinda.

Altunia was happy at this signal recognition but he
hated the idea of being separated from the Queen.
Hence, while thanking her for the great honour, he pro-
posed that they should get married.

" How can I, Altunia?" she asked. " I have yet to
put everything in order; in fact I do not know whom I
should trust and whom I should not. That is the reason
why I am sending you to Bhatinda; I want that part of
the empire to be in safe hands."

" But I am ready to go there even after we are married," said Altunia.

" Is it so easy for me to marry you?" asked Razia.
" Don't you understand what jealousies our marriage
would rouse among the other Amirs? Do you think our
troubles are over?"

" That means we shall never marry," said Altunia,
rather hopelessly.

" If that is what you feel then it means that you don't
have much faith in me or in my capacity to set things
right. I need time, Altunia. Please don't hustle me."

" Pray, don't misunderstand me, Razia. I do appreciate your difficulties. But we are young, we need each
other. How long are we to wait? This is as good a
time as any to be together. After all, we too must have
our share of happiness in life."

" True, but can't we wait for some time? For the
present I must concentrate on the affairs of state. There

are so many problems which need to be looked into. I have to put the whole empire in order. I am confident that soon we shall come out of the wood and establish peace and security in the realm. Then you will not find me so hesitant."

" I hope so, Razia."

" Oh, don't sound so cynical, Altunia," said Razia tenderly. " Do you really think that I don't want to be your wife? Do you doubt that I love you? You forget, Altunia, that I am a woman. The love of a woman is like the storm-swept sea, surging into eternity, while the love of a man is at best like an exotic flower, full of fragrance, but only so long as it lasts."

Soon after the departure of Altunia, Razia faced another challenge. It came from a most unexpected quarter. Learning of the insecure and unstable state of affairs in Delhi, the Kiramitah and Mulahidah sects among the Muslims gathered together from different parts of India under the leadership of a learned Turk named Nuruddin and marched to Delhi and encamped near the banks of the Jamuna. They vowed to be loyal to one another and to remain united against the orthodox sections—mostly belonging to the Hanafi and Shafi schools. Abusing their *ulema,* Nur the Turk—as Nuruddin came to be known—harangued his followers to rise against the Hanafis and the Shafis and to eliminate their hold on the palace.

They selected one Friday (March 5, 1237) to carry out their plan of usurping power. Arming themselves with swords and shields, more than a thousand of them entered the Juma Masjid—the main mosque of Islam in the capital—and fell upon the Muslims, who had gathered there for prayers. Panic gripped the worshippers and they began running helter skelter. Meanwhile, news of the attack reached the palace and a strong contingent of armed men arrived on the scene in time and attacked the invaders. The citizens also rose to the occasion and helped the imperial forces. Some Muslims, who had earlier, out of fright, run up to the roof of the Juma Masjid, poured down from there stones and bricks, hitting the trouble-makers.

Eventually the revolt was put down and Razia told the assembled crowd that fanaticism was at the root of all the trouble: first it encouraged a wrong approach towards non-Muslims and now it brought about dissensions in the ranks of the Muslims themselves. The various sects were the curse of Islam; in the name of religion they were teaching the Muslims not only to hate each other but also to isolate themselves from their fellow men. Razia reminded them that that was not the teaching of their Prophet; through love and understanding he wanted to unite human beings, not to divide them. Verily, he was a mercy to all mankind.

Razia's words had a profound effect on the gathering. Its anger vanished, the crowd dispersed peacefully, filled with admiration for the noble lady whom God had chosen to rule over them and who guided them so sagaciously and protected them so bravely.

11

THE SUNSHINE OF REFORMS

THUS fortified in her position, Razia decided to select from among the powerful Forty Amirs the more loyal ones, and to bestow her favours openly upon them. Ayaz and Altunia had already been singled out for special recognition, but others, even if not so close to the Queen, were also sought to be brought into her orbit of patronage provided they could be trusted to toe the line. The Queen was in no mood to tolerate any defiance of her authority from whatever quarter. Out of the ordeal of the past few months a new ruler had emerged, determined to assert herself. Her experience had, indeed, been bitter; it had convinced her that most of the Amirs were unworthy of the trust she had reposed in them so ungrudgingly, that they would betray her without the least compunction if an opportunity arose, and that, therefore, she should be more careful in future and less charitable towards not only the hostile but even the mercurial Amirs. Betrayal must not only be punished, but every care should be taken to guard against it. Furthermore sincerity must be rewarded and loyalty encouraged.

So reorienting her outlook, Razia proceeded to reshuffle her cabinet. She appointed as her Nizamul Mulk or Prime Minister Khwaja Muhazzabuddin, a

rather obscure Amir, who, Razia believed, would be too
grateful for the high honour to indulge in any intrigue
against her. She put the command of the army in the
hands of Saifuddin Aibak, a man of exceptional abilities,
" endowed ", as the official chronicle put it, " with diverse
manly qualities ".   Ikhtiyaruddin Aetigin—a handsome,
able and resourceful man with a dignified and regal bearing, but rather proud and self-centred—was made the
Amir-i-Hajib or the Lord Chamberlain. Similarly several
others were honoured including the pushing and highly
ambitious Balban, but he was made merely the Amir-i-
Akhur (lord of the stables) on the vacancy caused by the
promotion of the Abyssinian slave, Jamaluddin Yaqut,
whom Razia made, to the consternation of the Forty
Amirs, the Amirul Umra or the chief of the nobles, a
position which carried great privilege and extensive
patronage, never held before by anyone except a Turk
of the highest lineage.

Likewise, Razia made several changes in the various
governorships. Ayaz and Altunia had already been
posted to their respective charges. Though Tughril-i-
Tughan Khan—the former Comptroller of the Royal
Household and a good and generous man—did not help
Razia in suppressing the last rebellion, his non-participa-
tion on the side of the rebels was duly rewarded by his
being confirmed in his governorship of Lakhnawti with
additional status and authority. The province of Uch
was placed under Hindu Khan—a rather strange name
for the Mehtar-i-Mubarak or the auspicious chief, known
for his piety and orthodox way of life. The other Amirs
were equally rewarded, the more loyal receiving the better positions. In the words of a contemporary historian
—who was himself attached to the Imperial Court—
" from Debal to Lakhnawti all the Maliks and Amirs
manifested their obedience and submitted ".

By her consummate tact and ability Razia thus restored order and peace in most of the empire; only in Gwalior was there some trouble, caused by the death of Rashiduddin Ali, who was in command of its fortress; by seniority it devolved upon one Ziyauddin Ali, who was a kinsman of the fugitive Nizamul Mulk and hence ill disposed towards Razia. However, as soon as he showed signs of disaffection, the Queen instructed the neighbouring governor of Baren to proceed against him. On his arrival upon the scene with his forces, the former surrendered without a fight. He was directed to leave Gwalior for Delhi but he did not have the courage to face the Queen and went the same way as his notorious kinsman.

Meanwhile the growing power of Jajapellas (Yajvapala) posed a threat to the Sultanate. It assumed serious proportions when the ruler of Narwar, whom even the court chronicler describes as " the greatest of all the Rais of Hindustan ", raised the banner of revolt. He was, no doubt, checked but such was his defiance that it became impossible to suppress fully his rebellious behaviour.

Hence, in accordance with her declared policy of tolerance towards the Hindus, Razia ordered that the fortress at Gwalior be abandoned. The governor, thereupon, evacuated the troops, left the fortress and withdrew from the town.

The Forty Amirs reacted angrily; they called it an act of cowardice, though, in reality, it had been a masterstroke of leadership for the position of the imperial forces at Gwalior had become untenable. The Amirs were, however, convinced that Razia was in the wrong; furthermore they believed that if she showed such weakness in future the empire would be doomed.

Boldly and resolutely, Razia went ahead with her programme of imperial reconstruction. She spent a great deal of time and energy in giving relief to her subjects and in embarking on new measures to alleviate their sufferings. Often she went on visits to different parts of Delhi and the surrounding villages and saw for herself the pitiable conditions in which the poor lived. Decisive as always, she issued orders on the spot for the redress of their grievances. All this had a tremendous effect on the people and they prayed for her long life and continued prosperity.

The Queen also paid constant attention to the question of education and impressed upon the citizens of Delhi—among whom she became increasingly popular—the need for proper training both in religious subjects and military matters. She recalled from Gwalior the great scholar, Minhajus Seraj—who later wrote the celebrated *Tabakat-i-Nasiri*, describing the events of her times—and put him in charge of the famous Nasiri College, which, though founded by her father, was given a new impetus by Razia. She established other schools and employed many learned men as teachers there. Similarly in other literary fields the services of scholars were utilised. They were shown much respect and consideration at the Court. Towards musicians and painters also her attitude was extremely benevolent; she patronised them openly, some-times to the annoyance of her Amirs. There is said to be a painting of this period, in which Razia appears riding on her favourite horse. She had liked this work immensely and had rewarded the painter handsomely. So long as she reigned, it remained displayed in the hall of her durbar. Sensitive and enlightened, the Queen made no secret of her appreciation of arts and of artists; she also enjoyed the company of intellectuals, and gave them many opportunities for creative work.

Razia was particularly fond of open-air music, appro-priate to a procession or military display. At her court the military band played an important part. She allowed the different Amirs to have their own bands, the size of which depended on their rank. Some among the *ulema* did not like the encouragement given by her to music, but those were the days of the sufis or mystics in Islam who looked upon music as a means of realisation attained

through ecstasy. To her critics Razia gave the answer in the words of the great Muslim philosopher al-Ghazali: "Ecstasy means a state that comes from listening to music."

The Queen was not only a warm patron of the learned, who flocked to her court from far and near, but was herself deeply interested in every branch of knowledge. She gave a new dynamism to the intellectual development of the different races of her vast empire. Apart from schools, academies, research centres and public libraries were established, where the works of the great philosophers of former times were studied side by side with the Quran and the Traditions of the Prophet.

This was an age, when some of the greatest masterpieces of Arabic prose were written; elegant forms of belles-lettres held the literary field. In particular the Queen was charmed by the autobiographies of al-Ghazali and Usamah, the romantic writings of Ibn Tufail and the travelogue of Ibn Jubayr, for these represented a refreshingly new trend in Arabic literature.

But it was the renaissance of Persian culture which made the greatest impact on the Sultanate. The flowers of Persian prose and poetry adorned the intellectual garden in Delhi and enchanted the Turkish nobility, especially the fables of Saadi, the quatrains of Umar Khayyam and the poetic compositions of Firdausi and Nizami.

Moreover under Razia's patronage Aristotle, Plato, Euclid, Ptolemy and other Greek philosophers and savants received close attention; the Hindu treatises on sciences, philosophy, astronomy and literature were also given special recognition and included in the various courses in schools and colleges; despite some opposition from the *ulema*, Razia insisted that it was no shame to acknowledge and assimilate truth from whatever source it came, for truth, indeed, was universal and all-embracing. As an ancient Hindu text puts it:

The wisdom of the wise, the intellect
Of the informed, the greatness of the great,
The splendour of the splendid
To him who wisely sees,
The Brahman with his scrolls and sanctities,
The cow, the elephant, the unclean dog,
The outcaste gorging dog's meat, all are one.

Such was the broad humanism of the Queen who often listened with rapt attention to the commentaries that her scholars gave on the works of Ibn Sina and Ibn Rushd —the two great philosophers (the one from Iran and the other from Moorish Spain)—who had dilated with the accumulated wealth of ages on all the most important questions that occupied human attention and on which they had developed their own ideas with logical precision. She was especially impressed by Ibn Sina who had repudiated with indignation and contempt the charge of infidelity levelled against him by Muslim fanatics:

It is not easy to accuse me of heresy
My faith is firmer than any other faith
If in this world of yours
There is only one like me
And that one, a heretic,
Then there will not be a single Muslim in this world.

All in all, Razia, by her munificent patronage of scholarship and of the pursuit of the sciences and arts, had gathered round her a brilliant galaxy of savants and learned men in different fields of knowledge; they gave a new glory and added a fresh brilliance to her rule.

12

STRANGERS IN NEW ENVIRONMENT

By her enlightenment and liberalism Razia brought about so many changes in the character of the Sultanate that the old-fashioned Amirs felt themselves to be strangers in the new environment. They had lived under other rulers, including her father, the great Iltutmish, but never under a rule so alien to their temperament. The whole atmosphere was different; the learned were more respected than the Amirs; students were patronised instead of soldiers; and, to make matters worse, the Hindus were treated as if they were a part of the kingdom.

A new order took shape under which every subject, irrespective of race and creed, acquired the same rights—distinctions were done away with and disparities removed. The provisions of the penal code became applicable to all. Crimes were punished on the basis of evidence, and trial by ordeal was abolished. Likewise the civil law discouraged discriminations on grounds of sex, position, or wealth. Inter-provincial commerce flourished and contact with the outside world increased. In Razia's times, a traveller could freely pass " from the banks of the Indus to the Cilician gates ". She gave a new impetus to urban development; the gates of the cities were thrown open to artisans and workers. High and low resided in the same areas; consequently the tempo of progress increased. The lines of social distinctions became much less marked and the city boundaries developed as walls of defence, instead of as economic or social barriers. In the new cities, which grew up in the wake of this order, the poor and the down-trodden got enough work and their condition steadily improved. Trade multiplied tenfold and as a result of the centralisation of power there developed a uniform system of coinage, transport and communication. There was also a change in the technique of war; any able-bodied person could join the army and this altered not only the composition but also the character of the armed forces. Razia, moreover, encouraged the establishment of units of mounted fighters as against *paik* or foot soldiers. She took steps to build a strong standing army, recruited, paid and administered centrally.

In their heart of hearts, the Amirs did not like most of these measures. They saw in them the undermining of their feudal position and a systematic threat to their authority. Against some of these, they could not talk openly for they were patently beneficial to the Sultanate, but in regard to some others which benefited mainly the common people, they made no secret of their opposition. The Amirs decried these reforms in the name of Islam though neither their understanding of Islam nor knowledge of its tenets entitled them to speak in its name. They were in fact callow converts to the religion of Muhammad and functioned mainly in accordance with tribal greed and temporal instincts.

The truth apart, they exploited the religious sentiments and created problems for Razia. They branded the Hindus as Kafirs or infidels and pleaded that the Queen should show them no favours, for according to them such an approach was opposed to the larger interests of Islam.

To test them, Razia one day made the appointment of an Indian Muslim—a convert from Hinduism—Imamuddin Rayhan, as Wakif-i-Dar, an important office at the Court always held by a Turk. There was a tremendous furore among the Forty Amirs. After the *habshi* (negro), an Indian; this was too much for them. They met secretly and decided to protest to the Queen.

Balban led a delegation on their behalf; Razia could sense their feelings the moment they came to see her at the palace.

"Forgive us, Your Majesty," said Balban, with all humility, "but the Amirs are much upset! They feel you have no confidence in them."

"That is nonsense, Balban," replied the Queen. "Who can be more loyal to my kingdom than the Amirs! Without their support where would I be? They are the backbone of the empire. I trust them fully. Maybe sometimes I do things which may not be to their liking, but that has nothing to do with any lack of trust in them."

"Your Majesty, we admire the dynamism of your leadership; we respect the sincerity of your convictions; we appreciate your zeal for reforms; we are fully conscious of your great anxiety and burning desire to improve the lot of your subjects. But what is troubling us is the new appointment of an Indian as Wakif-i-Dar. Is there no Turk among your nobles to fill this post?"

"Of course, there are many among my Amirs. But I thought Rayhan is equally competent and worthy of our trust. He has served the empire well and he deserves some recognition."

"But he is an Indian, born of this soil and having no trace of Turkish blood in his veins."

" That may be, but he is a Muslim. ' All Muslims are brothers,' says the Quran. And you, my nobles, remind me of this text often."

" That is true. But it cannot apply to matters of state, Your Majesty. It is our privilege to occupy these high posts; they cannot be given to Indians."

" I see! So when it doesn't suit the Amirs, they can conveniently forget a Quranic injunction. I thought all your objections to my treatment of Hindu subjects arose from their not being Muslims. Now even Muslims, who are not Turks, are to be distrusted."

" We do believe that all Muslims are brothers, but where is it said in the Quran, Your Majesty, that they are all equal?"

" I thought the whole basis of Islam was equality of brotherhood."

" In that case why was the family of Quresh—the Prophet's family—considered the highest in Arabia?"

" That was before the advent of Islam. The Prophet did away with all these distinctions."

" But soon after his death they came to the fore again for this is inherent in human nature. As Your Majesty is aware, the members of the Prophet's family—the Syeds as they came to be known—continued to enjoy the highest position; in fact they became a new nobility in the eyes of the people of Islam."

" That was on the spiritual and religious plane. Your objection to my appointment of Rayhan is purely temporal and tribal."

" It is the tribe, Your Majesty, which is the strength of our empire."

" And do you think the appointment of one Indian Muslim to just one of the many offices is going to shake that empire?"

" It may not, Your Majesty, but once a wedge is driven into our closely-knit circle, it may be difficult to stop the process. That is why we have to be careful."

" All right, Balban, I grant you your wish! I have no desire to displease the Amirs on a matter like this. I thought the bond of Islam was strong enough for you to accept Imamuddin Rayhan as one of us. It would have strengthened the basis of our rule. But prejudices die hard and we are all too self-centred to see beyond the nose. After all, Rayhan will have to work with the Amirs and, since they do not like his appointment, it is better, in his own interest, that I cancel his appointment."

Balban and the other Amirs who had accompanied him made obeisance to the Queen and left the palace. Though they had won their point, they knew that the Queen was not happy; she had seen through their game. The real issue was different: who was to rule, the Queen, according to her lights, or the Amirs, according to their ambitions? As they went out of the Palace, Balban warned them that unless they were vigilant about their rights, they would lose all their power. Razia, he said, was no ordinary ruler; she was an astute politician, who knew how to weather any storm. The longer she stayed on the throne the stronger would be her hold. She might allow the Amirs to have their way here and there, but, as Balban explained to his compatriots, she was aiming much higher—at the establishment of the unchallenged supremacy of her authority.

But what should be done to check her—that was their big problem. She had strengthened the empire, improved the administration and brought peace and security to the realm. The people were happy under her rule and the situation on the whole had taken a turn for the better. At the time of her accession, Razia had pro-

mised that if she did not prove better than any man, she could be deposed; but, even Balban, with all his ingenuity and cleverness, could not establish such a proposition against her.   In ability she had no equal; in popularity, no rival; in administration, no peer.

However, Razia suffered, according to Balban, from one weakness—her excessive fondness for the Abyssinian slave, Jamaluddin Yaqut, who had grown from strength to strength—much to the chagrin of the Amirs—ever since she had made him the Amir-i-Akhur.   The close relationship between the two was not hidden from the Amirs.   But Balban suspected that there was something illicit about it.   Their riding together every morning, their frequent meetings during any hour of the day at the palace and above all the many favours bestowed on Yaqut by the Queen were all indicative of an intimacy between the two which Balban was not prepared to accept as mere friendship.   It was something more; it was, he believed, a sinful relationship.   But how to establish the charge? Balban pondered over the matter for days together but could not come to a decision. To spread a scandal against the Queen was bad enough; but to spread a scandal of such dimensions could shake the Sultanate. On the other hand, if Balban kept quiet he would miss the opportunity of a lifetime to usurp power. The dilemma was not only real but terrible; Balban was afraid of its repercussions, no doubt, but he still wanted to face it. He was aware that in case he failed he would have to pay the price with his life, for the people would not tolerate such an aspersion on the character of their beloved Queen; moreover, it could endanger greatly the position of the Forty Amirs. Astute as he was, Balban was conscious of these risks; but ambition had the better of him; it gave him no rest; it plagued his mind constantly.

Of late he and Malik Aitegin had come closer to each other. They shared many thoughts and they agreed on many points. Balban decided, therefore, to take Aitegin into his confidence. At first hesitantly and then more openly, he divulged his suspicion to the lord chamberlain. To Balban's surprise he found his friend all ears. He wanted to know more and more about the whole affair. The two of them discussed it at length but decided to go about it cautiously; without directly involving themselves they agreed that they should encourage its exposure to others. At first only the Queen's enemies would be taken into confidence; then, slowly, other influential persons would be told. Silently and secretly, the scandal would be spread far and wide, until it reached all ears. In the meantime, however, the utmost caution would be exercised. This was the time when Razia's popularity was at its zenith; her subjects simply adored her; any slur on her character was bound to enrage them, leading even to the elimination of her traducers. Fully aware of these consequences, both Balban and Aitegin decided to play safe. All that they would do was to study the situation, to lie low for some time, and then make use of the opportune moment, if and when it came.

13

THE PRICE OF A CROWN

MEANWHILE Razia went ahead with her plans to consolidate the empire. Between her and the new Nizamul Mulk there developed good understanding. She treated him with respect and consideration and he was all obedience to her. There were, no doubt, frequent meetings with the Forty Amirs and even discussions on matters of policy, but these did not help to create an atmosphere of cordiality. There was no love lost between the two sides, and as time passed the estrangement widened. The Amirs could not be enthused about the welfare of the common people, and Razia was dedicated to that cause. They believed in maintaining their own hegemony, while Razia desired greater integration between the rulers and the ruled. While the Amirs were parochial and sectarian in their outlook, the Queen was broad-minded and humanitarian. Hence the very basis for a closer understanding between them did not exist; they just tolerated each other.

One day the Nizamul Mulk informed Razia that the Forty Amirs did not like the interest she was taking in scholars and intellectuals and felt unhappy at their growing influence at the court. The Queen reminded him that, of all the attributes that a ruler should possess, knowledge must take precedence. Quoting the Prophet she said that he had enjoined upon his followers the acquiring of knowledge so that the possessor might distinguish right from wrong and be able to guide others in good pursuits and give them proper leadership.

" But the Amirs feel that they must have precedence over these scholars," pointed out the Nizamul Mulk.

" Why? They cannot be their equals. As the Quran has said, ' And the blind and the seeing are not alike; nor darkness nor light; nor the cool shade or the hot wind ' "

As time passed, Razia became still more assertive, and the impact of her personality began to be felt in every sphere. The leading Amirs, including Balban and Aitegin, decided that the Queen must be curbed. If they could not bend her to their own will, they had to break her.

Though shrewd and worldly-wise, Razia remained blissfully ignorant of these developments. She did not suspect that soon after one revolt the Forty Amirs would be conspiring to prepare for another. About some she had her suspicions—of them the most prominent was Ayaz, the egocentric and ambitious governor of Lahore. On him she kept a vigilant watch, but the rest seemed harmless, particularly because, she thought, they were too selfish to invite retaliation. However, she misjudged Balban, whose bluntness she mistook for straightforwardness. Also she admired his ability; that was why she bestowed many favours on him and gave him much importance at the court. Little did she imagine that he would be the chief instrument of her destruction. Similar was the case of some other Amirs who owed their high positions to her. She had shown them respect and given them no affront. But men are strange creatures; they find it difficult to accept a woman as an equal, much less as a superior. This prejudice blinds them to all

other considerations. Particularly so in the case of
Razia, for the Forty Amirs, by and large, were afraid of
her increasing hold on the affairs of the empire and jealous of her growing popularity.

Again, what piqued them was the Queen's friendship
with the negro, Jamaluddin Yaqut, who had become her
constant companion. Apart from their frequent meetings, many people knew that they enjoyed each other's
company and shared each other's thoughts. Though
the ties between the two were not of recent origin,
they had of late become much stronger. The Queen was
aware that her attitude towards Yaqut had created jealousy among the other Amirs. But what could she do?
Being human, she needed to relax now and then, especially when the cares of state exhausted her. It was different
when Altunia was in Delhi; he had filled the vacuum;
but he was now the governor of Bhatinda—far away from
the capital. Yaqut therefore became almost a habit with
her.

" I am becoming more and more fond of you, Yaqut,"
one day Razia confided to the Abyssinian.

" Allah be praised, my noble lady, for I know not
what I have done for this blessing," Yaqut said.

" I think the Amirs are not happy. They look at our
relationship with suspicion."

" What can they suspect?" asked Yaqut innocently.

" I don't know, but men are a suspicious lot. My
Amirs, in particular, have not reconciled themselves to
the position I have given you. They attribute it to our
friendship. They think you have a personal hold on
me."

" I don't know of any hold that I have over you, but
I do know this—that my life is at your command," submitted Yaqut with all sincerity.

" The two of us have been together for so long, Yaqut,

that a strange bond—strong and unbreakable—has developed between us. I cannot deny it."

"You mean everything to me, my noble lady. When I am in your presence I feel elevated. I don't know much about love, but my devotion to you is full and complete in every respect."

"I am conscious of it and I have no words to thank you for it. There is something about you which moves me deeply. Sometimes when you look at me a great warmth wells up inside me. At such moments I wish I were not a Queen."

"But even a Queen is human."

"Yes, she is human but so utterly helpless as far as her own happiness is concerned."

"How can a Queen be helpless?"

"She is, if she is conscientious and cares for the welfare of her people."

"But will Your Majesty never think of yourself? Who are these Amirs? They can be finished off in no time. The soldiers are with us; the people are with us."

"But the Amirs are the leaders, who really matter."

"Do they, really? It is of such leaders that al-Mutanabbi wrote:

The men of our time lack greatness
Although they have power in their hands

These men are no more than rabbits,
But they pretend to be kings."

"How well the poet has spoken; but these Amirs must not be allowed to mislead my subjects. That is why I must be careful."

"But, believe me, Your Majesty, your subjects love you. They will always stand by you."

" I doubt, Yaqut, whether they would, if they knew that their Queen has fallen in love with an Abyssinian."

" Forgive me, my Queen, but is Razia, of all persons, becoming a coward?"

" No, Yaqut, but what can valour do in the face of deep-rooted prejudice?"

" So we have to pander to the whims of others!"

" That is the price a Queen must pay, Yaqut."

" Or is it Altunia who is the real cause?"

" Since you have mentioned Altunia I must be frank with you. My love for him is no less sincere and deep, Yaqut. Altunia and I have always thought of ourselves as a pair; even the Amirs know that one day we shall be married. I know Altunia is ambitious; but, with all his faults, he inspires a peculiar faith in me which is not easily shaken."

" But you don't love him?"

" I don't know. I am so confused. Frankly I am as fond of him as I am of you. But the two of you move me differently. I cannot tear myself away from either of these attachments."

" But that is wrong, Your Majesty. You cannot love two persons at one and the same time!"

" I am not sure of the morality of my feelings. Perhaps you are right in saying that I should be more decisive. O, Yaqut, I am so confused. Tell me, am I doing something terribly wrong?"

" Please don't reproach yourself. You are a woman in a million—the purest of the pure. No evil thought can ever enter your mind."

" Though I feel so strongly, Yaqut, I am still afraid to let my heart have the better of me for I think that to be prudent and to love is not given to human beings!"

" I understand you perfectly, but I hope Your Majesty does not propose to marry Altunia."

"I don't know, Yaqut? After all marriage with Altunia will create far fewer problems. The Amirs may be jealous of Altunia but eventually they will accept my marriage with him. He is a bird of the same feather."

"And I am black. That is why you will not marry me."

"Aren't you being unfair to me? Was I talking about my attitude, or that of the Amirs?"

And with a twinkle in her eyes Razia added, "Don't you know that black men are pearls in ladies' eyes?"

Yaqut smiled and said, "But the Amirs hate me and Your Majesty desires that we must bow to their desire."

"For the sake of the unity and integrity of the empire, how can I ignore their wishes on such a vital matter?"

"I don't care, my Queen, for myself or for my feelings. I am all yours for whatever I am worth."

"I know that, Yaqut, and that is why there is this conflict in my mind."

After some time Yaqut left and Razia retired to her bed-chamber. She could not sleep for a long time that night, wondering what kind of a woman she was. Both Altunia and Yaqut meant so much to her; but neither claimed her heart completely. Both left some emptiness in her. Strangely enough she felt a strong emotional entanglement with both of them. She could be free like a bird with Yaqut, but with Altunia, despite their fondness for each other, there was a peculiar barrier—or rather a feeling of restraint, which was none the less ennobling. She would never want to break it. Altunia was cast in a different mould and perhaps as a life companion he would prove much better than Yaqut. But Yaqut was in many respects a fascinating person, a lovable creature, who moved every fibre of her being!

And so the Queen remained in a state of indecision. The more she thought, the more confused she became.

Though decisive by nature, she found herself utterly
helpless in face of this important problem of her life. It
made her more unhappy, adding to the pangs of her
loneliness. She tried, consequently, to suppress personal frustration by concentrating on her work more
and more. From dawn to dusk she kept herself busy,
looking into her correspondence, answering important
letters, holding deliberations with her prime minister
and council of ministers and meeting with intellectuals,
scholars and artists and going round the streets of Delhi
to see for herself how the poorer sections of her subjects
lived. All these activities occupied much of her time;
in them she found a certain satisfaction. When she grew
very weary from affairs of state, she relaxed in the company of Yaqut, riding with him to the outskirts of the
capital or just being together at the palace, humming
to him the verses of Rumi, the rising poet of mysticism
in Islam:

Happy the moment when we are seated in the palace,
  thou and I,
With two forms and with two figures but with one
  soul, thou and I.

Those were moments when she lived in a different
world—when everything around, the changing seasons,
the earth and the sky, the trees and the flowers, the moun-
tains and the landscapes, moved her in many mysterious
ways. Often she looked forward to these moments to
drown her loneliness; but with her cautiousness, it could
at best be merely an escape.

But escape is no solution; sometimes, in consequence,
she turned to a more spiritual environment to gain peace
of mind. Those were the days of the sufis and saints in
India; she visited their shrines and listened to their dis-

courses. Once as a mark of appreciation, Razia sent
some gold to a leading sufi, for whom she had the highest
regard. Though he led an extremely austere life and
managed on a *dang* (or silver coin) a day, which his freed
slaves gave him, the saint was angry with the Queen.
How did she dare to insult him by throwing such wordly
crumbs to him? He beat with sticks the royal messenger
who had brought the gold and sent him back. As soon
as Razia heard of the episode she realised what inner
strength the saint possessed; in comparison how weak
and involved was she! In her restlessness, she com-
muned with her own heart and remained still for hours.

14

FIGHTER AND DIPLOMAT

DESPITE the adventurous climate of the times and the full bloom of her youth, Razia was an embodiment of restraint. She loathed recklessness; cool and collected always, she pondered over every move before deciding

on a particular course of action. At times, the Amirs were exasperated at this attitude, but more often than not the events justified it. However, she rarely showed weakness; where firmness was needed she was not found wanting.

For days together, Razia tolerated many of the hostile acts of the governor of Lahore, Malik Izzuddin Ayaz, but as soon as she realised that he was posing a real threat to the Sultanate, she fought him with a relentlessness which surprised the Amirs. The rebel governor was chased so fiercely that he had to escape towards the frontier. The Royal forces were commanded by the Queen herself and the manner in which she led the attack was a tribute to her military genius. From whichever side the harassed Malik tried to flee, he was blocked; only the Chenab border was left open for him. He took to his heels in that direction but as soon as he crossed that border, he was confronted by the Mongols. Exhausted and tired, the governor surrendered to the royal forces. He was brought like a fugitive before the Queen.

" Tell me, Ayaz," asked Razia, " what should I do to you?"

Kneeling and with folded hands, the old and bearded governor said, " Have mercy on me, Your Majesty!"

" Do you deserve it? How many times in the past have I not forgiven you. You were instrumental in breaking the will of the Sultan and depriving me of the throne. But when I became the Queen I forgave you. Then you organised the rebellion against me in the capital. I again forgave you and as soon as you began co-operating with me, I made you the governor of the most important province of Lahore. You are too ambitious to be contained."

" I don't know what came over me, Your Majesty. I admit you have been more than generous to me. To all your Amirs you have been good, but towards me you have been particularly kind and indulgent."

"And you showed your gratitude by rebelling against me once again!"

"I deserve death, Your Majesty, but I beseech your mercy."

"You shall have it, Ayaz; but it will not cure you. The trouble with you is that you are disgustingly ambitious. The more you have the more you want. I gave you position; I gave you power; I showed you respect; but instead of being grateful you rose against me. You wanted to be independent of me so that you could rule like a Sultan. It is Amirs like you who are the real danger to the stability and integrity of our empire. I have, however, no heart to behead you. I only hope that my forgiveness will shame you into a better realisation of your duties to your ruler, who will always be able to crush you if you ever try and raise the banner of revolt again."

"I swear by Allah that I shall always be loyal to Your Majesty!"

"Persons like you have no faith, Ayaz. Their oaths have no meaning. They know not what repentence is, but still I would not like to stain my hands with your blood. I pity you, Ayaz. When I look at you, I am reminded of what the great poet, Abu Shukur of Balkh, has said:

The tree which bears a bitter fruit
Being nurtured by delicacies and sweets
Will not change its nature
It will bear the same bitter fruit
And you will not taste from it any sweetness."

Razia ordered her troops to set free the Malik but he was shorn of his insignia of office. The action did not please many of her supporters, who believed that only deterrent punishment could succeed in checking such acts of hostility against the throne. However, Razia was constituted differently; with all her qualities as a ruler, she had a woman's heart. She could never be ruthless; she forgave her enemies with a generosity rare in her times; she harboured ill will against none; on the contrary, she was only too willing to forgive and forget. Amiable by nature and kind and gentle of disposition she loved to generate good will all round; as a ruler she believed that contented and happy subjects constituted the greatest bulwark of her rule.

In the art of diplomacy also Razia had few equals. Her father, the great Iltutmish, had trained her in its intricacies. He had been a past master in that art, but the pupil proved to be equally proficient.

One day without any prior intimation, Hasan Qarlugh, an ex-Khwarizmi governor of Ghazni, came to Delhi and sought the Queen's help against the Mongols, who had dispossessed him of his territory. He had been a good friend of Iltutmish and had helped him to check the Mongol forces on the frontiers of the Sultanate. He was, therefore, hopeful of enlisting Razia's help.

"Your Majesty, it was the friendship between your illustrious father and myself that checked the Mongol forces at that time from advancing into India and saved the Sultanate."

"I know that very well, Your Highness. Our dynasty is ever so grateful to you."

"But I need your help now; united we can defeat the Mongol forces, which are much weaker now than they were in the days of your great father."

" I am sorry to hear of what these barbarians have done
to you, Your Highness, despite your acceptance of their
suzerainty.   They should have treated you, on the contrary, with respect and consideration," said the Queen.

" I am one of the Khwarizmis who have been the
enemies of the Mongols for so many years.   They could
not trust me.   And I don't blame them.   That is why,
in my hour of need, I have come to a friend," explained
the former Governor.

Razia assured him that she would do all she could to
help him; but she had to consult the Forty Amirs.
Hasan Qarlugh pleaded with her to be prompt and Razia
assured him that she would give the most urgent consideration to his request.   She ordered that the ex-gover-
nor be treated as her personal guest.   He was shown all
respect and given all comforts.   In his honour banquets
were held, parades organised, and lavish receptions given.

To consider his request, Razia called immediately a
meeting of the Forty Amirs and explained the situation
to them.   But they were too scared of the invincible
Mongols to agree to any alliance against them.   Razia
put forward the case of Hasan Qarlugh as effectively as
she could, but she had known beforehand that the
Amirs, enjoying the ease and comfort of life in Delhi,
would be in no mood to undertake such a hazardous
responsibility.

" The Mongols are tough; they are ruthless; they
believe in fighting to the last.   What is the sense in
provoking them?" asked Aitegin, the lord chamberlain.

" I think it will be madness on our part to entertain
any such request," said Balban.   " The Mongols are not
troubling us.   Why should we invite trouble on our
heads?"

" To help a friend," replied the Queen.

" That is asking too much," said the Naib-i-Lashkar, Saifuddin Aibak.

" Isn't it a strange attitude on the part of the head of our forces?" Razia asked, rather sternly.

" I am sorry, Your Majesty, but I am only being realistic. Even your great father never provoked the Mongols; the Khwarizmians tried to involve him on their side and to make him fight with the Mongols, but the Sultan managed to hold himself aloof, and thus kept the Mongols from our borders."

The durbar over, the Queen conveyed the reaction of the Forty Amirs to Hasan Qarlugh. He was utterly disappointed. He pressed Razia not to let her down; but the Queen expressed her helplessness. Qarlugh argued that she could overrule the Amirs and join him but Razia explained that it would not help him. Unless the Amirs were solidly behind her, how could the Mongols be repelled? Theirs was an invincible might; a divided and half-hearted enemy could prove no match to it. Moreover, Razia explained, " I don't believe, Your Highness, in either provoking the enemy or taking precipitate action against him."

" That is not the point, Your Majesty. We must strike before it is too late."

" That is what your Shah did, and what did he achieve? He felt that putting to death the envoys of Gengis Khan would frighten the old warrior, but instead it led to the destruction of the Shah's own empire, which had become so progressive under his leadership."

" Perhaps the Shah should have been more discreet, but do you think the fight could have been avoided?"

" At least the Shah would have been better prepared."

" Gengis Khan was a genius, Your Majesty. Though our Shah fought him bravely—the Mongol himself said of the Shah that ' such a son a father must have '—he could not possibly defeat him. But the sons of the mighty Khan are quarrelling among themselves and now is our opportunity to strike at them and finish them off."

" I am not so sure, Your Highness. The empire that Gengis Khan has left behind cannot be disrupted so soon, for it has been built by the sweat and blood of his people, who, though short in stature, are sturdy of limb. They are valiant and daring, ever ready to jump into any peril at a signal from their commander. Moreover, they are better trained and equipped now, with finer and more effective armour, and I would, therefore, not like to involve ourselves in a fight with them. That is my honest feeling, Your Highness."

Razia's sincerity and frankness had a deep effect on Hasan Qarlugh. He realised that retaliation against the Mongols might result in more death and destruction. He had come to the Queen, full of anger and hate; he returned sober, and convinced that discretion was better than valour. At the time of his departure, Razia assigned to him, as a gesture of friendship and in appreciation of his understanding, the revenue of Bazam for his personal expenses.

15

THE TWILIGHT AND THE DUST

THREE years had passed since Razia's accession to the throne, three years of trial and tribulation, stress and strain, in which she had faced all kinds of challenges to her authority. But her tact and ability in managing the affairs of the Sultanate and her abounding self-confidence had helped the Queen to consolidate her position. Though a woman, with all the delicacy and weakness of her sex, she had proved to be a remarkable ruler.

Whether as a commander on the battlefield or as an administrator in the secretariat or as a social reformer among the people she did not fail to make her mark. She had vision and foresight, the boldness to take decisions and the courage to implement them; withal, nature had endowed her with a pleasing disposition and the rarest of all gifts—the gift of winning the hearts of her subjects. In the annals of history there have been many reigning queens, but Razia stands out as one of the finest exemplars of her kind. She had all the attributes of a ruler—in particular she gave her subjects a warmth of devotion, and a singleness of dedication, which a woman alone, at her best, could give.

The Amirs had not bargained for such a Queen. In a moment of crisis they had agreed to her accession, little realising that Razia, by her qualities of head and heart, would be a threat to their feudal and reactionary approach. Step by step, and with a sincerity of purpose that startled friend and foe alike, she tried to change the whole pattern of the Sultanate. Instead of deriving her strength from the Forty Amirs, she created a new reservoir of goodwill for herself among the people, both Hindus and Muslims, both high and low. For them the Queen became " the shadow of God on earth ", not only in name but in reality. In the manner of her administration—the reforms, the popular contacts, the public dispensation of justice—Razia lived up to their best expectations. She became to her subjects the very embodiment of their hopes and aspirations.

To dislodge such a Queen was no easy task; it could unleash a revolution. And still the Forty Amirs were adamant in their determination. Balban and Aitegin had succeeded in convincing them that there was no other alternative if they were not to lose their power and position. Consequently, they hatched a plot to carry out their design. It was done so secretly that Razia did not have the slightest inkling of it—or when she had an inkling of it, it was too late.

And the plot was one of the meanest that could have been devised by the human mind. It was to make the least suspected of the Amirs—Altunia—who was politically the nearest to Razia and personally in love with her, to revolt against her. The method adopted was to poison his ears assiduously and effectively in regard to the alleged illicit relationship between Razia and Yaqut. At first the governor of Bhatinda refused to believe the story, but when his trusted friend, Aitegin, vouchsafed for it, the seed of suspicion was successfully sown in Altunia's mind. To nurture it, reports were sent of the daily meetings between the Queen and Yaqut through Altunia's own men, who gave the Amir graphic descriptions of how the two met, where they met and how long they met. These had, naturally, a terrible effect on the already susceptible mind of Altunia. His jealousy aroused, he was caught in the grip of anger and revenge. Also he felt humiliated and betrayed. To avenge his honour he decided to fall in line with Balban and Aitegin in their sinister design to oust Razia from the throne.

As planned, Altunia raised the banner of revolt at Bhatinda and declared his severance from Delhi.

When Razia heard of it, she was shocked beyond measure. How could he do this to her? He, of all persons, who had always protested his love for her and assured her that he would stand by her to the last! Were men so base and mean? Could no one among them be trusted? A woman was despised because she was weak and fickle-minded; but would the worst among women have fallen so low? Completely disillusioned, Razia decided to meet the new challenge posed by Altunia. Though tired and exhausted from her journey to Lahore, where only a short time before she had brought Ayaz to his knees, she prepared herself to battle against Altunia. She had returned to Delhi on March 15, 1240, and now, on April 3, she had to leave the capital again. The royal forces were mobilised once more under her personal command and the march to Bhatinda began, with Yaqut as her chief lieutenant.

It was the month of Ramzan—the month of fasting. The weather was unbearably hot and the journey from Delhi to Bhatinda long and arduous. But Razia was too upset by Altunia's action to postpone the march. For once she lost her balance and the personal hurt she felt warped her political judgment.

At the outset of the march, the soldiers were full of life; but soon the rigours of the fasting and of the heat began to tell on them. They kept up their spirit, but the flesh, being weak, gave in. As they neared the battle-ground they were worn out. The journey indeed turned out to be an ordeal.

Meanwhile, Aitegin and Balban engaged themselves in preparations in the capital. Already they had planned the broad outline of their action. They now anxiously waited for the signal from Altunia. On receiving word of Razia's surrender they were to take steps to proclaim as ruler her brother, Behram. Armed soldiers, loyal to Aitegin and Balban, were posted at strategic points. They would crush any manifestation of loyalty to Razia. Every detail was worked out; all eventualities were anti-cipated, for Balban did not believe in leaving anything to chance; thorough and methodical, he had arranged to meet every situation. His friend, Aitegin, as the accepted leader of the coup, was, however, a little ner-vous. Lacking Balban's self-confidence, he held his breath as he waited for the crucial hour.

Hardly had they reached Bhatinda, when Razia's forces met Altunia's on the battlefield. The encounter took place on one of the hottest days of the season. The rays of the sun had scorched the soldiers; the march across long and weary distances, through difficult and inacces-sible tracts, had sapped their energy. They could not, therefore, give a good account of themselves. They, however, fought with fierce tenacity, but the soldiers of Altunia, who were fresh, vigorous and better organised, had the better of them. And then something happened which shattered Razia's last hope: Altunia's soldiers concentrated on Yaqut, hunted him out and cut him to pieces. That was their revenge on a man, who, they believed, had stabbed their master, Altunia, in the back.

The news produced the most demoralising effect on Razia's soldiers. The Queen tried to hold them together, but to no avail. One battalion after another surrendered. Only the one under her direct command put up a grim and brave fight, but the odds against her were too heavy. Finally Razia was captured—the first defeat she ever suffered, and that too at the hands of the man who had proclaimed his unbounded love for her. Such was the irony of fate!

Altunia no doubt showed the utmost respect to the Queen—she was interned in a palatial mansion and given all comforts. But Razia was too restless a soul to enjoy life behind bars.

As al-Hamdani wrote:

Oh, hard captivity!
Oh, dark, unending, starless nights!
How slowly these hours pass,
And they are not pleasant to bear!

The death of Yaqut had also been a great blow; it grieved her greatly. One day, in a supreme moment of sorrow and dejection, she broke down and burst into tears, remembering the moving verses of Ibn al-Farid, whose poetry is a model of ecstatic inspiration:

Though he be gone, mine every limb beholds him
In every charm and grace and loveliness;
In music of the lute and the flowing reed,
Mingled in consort with melodious airs;
And in green hollows where in cool of eve
Gazelles roam browsing, or at break of morn;
And where the gathered clouds let fall their rain
Upon a flowery carpet woven of blooms.

The more she brooded the more depressed she became.
How could this happen? How could Altunia, of all
persons, behave like this?   Again and again these questions disturbed her, and she could find no answer to
them. Her imagination became blurred; it proved of
no assistance; even her cool comprehension failed to
soothe her.   Razia had experienced enough ingratitude;

but such a betrayal shook her entire being. There must have been some deep-rooted plot, some large-scale organisation, but she knew nothing about it. Nor was she aware of the principal instigators or main actors, nor of the details of the plot. She reproached herself for being so gullible—for relying on friends so blindly. But if friends failed, what could a Queen do? And such trusted friends! Razia's only hope lay in the dissensions that might follow among the Forty Amirs. She knew that the distribution of the spoils of office among these men were bound to shatter their unity. In case they quarrelled, jealousies would be roused and new alignments forged. Then would be the time for Razia to retrieve her glory and power.

But as a prisoner of Altunia what could she do? She was cut off from the rest of the world. She had no news of the happenings in the capital. Everywhere there was disillusionment and she groped in the dark. And still she hoped against hope that something would happen to rescue her from her humiliation. Her subjects would rise; her supporters would revolt. How could she be thrown away so easily? Razia thought over the past; she worried about the future. Anxiously she waited for a ray of hope, but none appeared. Her world seemed to have come to an end.

And then some unexpected development took place in Delhi. As already decided by the Forty Amirs, as soon as the news of Razia's capture reached the capital, her younger brother, Behram, was proclaimed the Sultan. Aitegin, as the chief conspirator, became the Naib-i-Mamlikat, or Deputy of the Realm, wielding all executive powers. At a hurriedly organised coronation, the other Amirs, including Balban, were given important offices. All those suspected of the slightest loyalty to

Razia were either put to death or deprived of their position or status. The revenge was complete.

But as the months passed, many Amirs became jealous of the growing power of Aitegin; even the friendship between him and Balban cooled off. The two could easily conspire together against Razia, but, as ambitious men both, they found that they could not remain friends in power. Either could rule; both could not. Balban proved to be the more cunning. He managed to poison the ears of the new Sultan against Aitegin; the ruler also became alarmed at the increasing assumption of power by his deputy. Aitegin began keeping an elephant—a prerogative of the King—and playing the *naubat* at the gates of his palace.

He also married one of the divorced sisters of the Sultan. One suspicion followed another; these added up to a heap of mistrust. Balban conspired, therefore, with the Sultan to do away with Aitegin. One day two hefty and strong-muscled Turks were commissioned by them to stab the deputy to death as he came down from the upper storey of the Qasr-i-Sufan, after he had participated in a Muharram meeting. The act was committed so casually that it stunned the Amirs, but since they were themselves jealous of the growing power of Aitegin, it produced no reaction. Balban was not, however, able to step into the deceased's shoes. He had to wait a few more years before he could wield the supreme authority, which he was to do, first for twenty years, as the Naib-i-Mamlikat or deputy to the pious and unassuming Sultan Nasiruddin Mahmud (who married Balban's daughter), and later by himself assuming the crown of the Sultanate. Instead, the King appointed the Amir, Badruddin Rumi, as the new Naib-i-Mamlikat.

Altunia expected high rewards from the new Sultan for his services in bringing about Razia's downfall almost single-handedly, but he waited in vain. The Amirs in Delhi distributed the offices among themselves; they were too concerned about their own selves to bother about an outsider. Altunia had-faith in Aitegin, who had assured him that, as soon as the new regime settled down, the governor of Bhatinda would receive the rewards due to him. The death of Aitegin, therefore, came as a stunning blow to Altunia. He lost all hope in the Sultan and in the Amirs, and decided to act without any further loss of time.

He began visiting Razia in the prison. The Queen did not know why, but she did not resent his overtures. Encouraged, he became all tenderness to her; his chivalrous behaviour enlivened the relationship. The two met often now, and though they talked at first with some reserve their meetings turned out to be meaningful. Soon these gave rise to the illusion of a common rhythm, which could inspire a new determination to overcome all obstacles, and led to an awareness of the need for unity, which, if accomplished, could turn the tide. Whether that unity was the product of circumstances or the fusion of two hearts it was difficult to say. But in the supreme crisis, which the one created for the other, destiny once again brought them together. They had, therefore, no choice but to turn their back on the past, refusing to allow it to spoil their present or to ruin their future. At that moment they realised that each needed the other. Thus circumstances, undreamt of by either, forged the marital tie between the Queen and her betrayer. Strange, indeed, are the tricks which the wheel of fate plays upon human beings!

16

THE AGONY OF DEFEAT

"WHAT a glorious morning," said Razia to Altunia, after she had spent a night for the first time out of prison walls. There was the same aristocratic tone of voice and accent which was so habitual with the Queen; but the upsurge of new emotions had somewhat changed the expression on her face, which began to show the same splendour as before. Relaxed and much less disturbed, she felt lifted and impelled by an inner rhythm, with fresh—albeit soft and subdued—music playing in her heart.

Altunia responded as harp to harp, though the two were poles apart by nature. Razia was the picture of calmness and sobriety; Altunia—though less impetuous now—had still the same dash and verve. They were to be joined together in marriage, but more important to both was their political future. They had lost much of the bond which had tied them in the past, but they comforted themselves with the thought that each could be the salvation of the other. In unity was their strength.

Their supporters were also happy. Singly the two could not fight the Centre; together they might humble it. The brilliance of the combination dazzled their people; a combination of two forces such as these, they believed, could subjugate the old world and build a new one.

The people were, therefore, much excited about the marriage. It promised to be the harbinger of a glorious fulfilment. Preparations were made on a grand scale for the event had to be exploited politically. Thousands of people—big and small, important and unimportant—from far and near came for the ceremony. From the bottom of their hearts they blessed the couple, for the alliance represented, in every sense, the best of Turkish nobility.

Though the wedding formalities ended in the calm of the occasion, it was not without tension. The past still cast its shadow on the relationship. Razia no doubt looked happy, but she wondered whether the marriage would work, whether the right basis for it had been laid. Altunia in his new-found happiness looked a titan of confidence and energy. When Razia looked at him as her bridegroom, she felt his magic spell. Clutching at Altunia's arms, she came close to him. He drew her nearer. Suddenly Razia tried to free herself, but Altunia held her tight.

" Razia! Let us forget the past and start a new life," he implored.

The Queen did not reply. The ensuing silence was like a pause between two eternities. Then suddenly she rushed to him. He put his arms round her and caressed her.

For both Razia and Altunia a new life began. He realised how grievously he had wronged the Queen. What nobility, what sincerity, what understanding she possessed! In her company Altunia became overwhelmingly gentle, developing a new respect for her.

The next few days were taken up in celebration of the marriage. The banquet hall was arranged with all the splendour that the wealth of Bhatinda could provide. The guests included the scions of the noblest families, the commanders of the forces, the heads of different establishments. Razia looked resplendent in her bridal robes and jewels. Nothing pleased Altunia more than to strut about as the protector of the daughter of Iltutmish and as the husband of the Queen of India. Proudly he exclaimed, in the hearing of the assembled gentry, " Soon we shall start on our journey to take back the throne of Delhi!"

Quietly Razia looked at him and saw in his eyes a fiery brilliance which she had never seen in any man before. At that moment she understood how determined he was. But she preferred to wait until the enemy's plan revealed itself. Though information was hard to obtain and Altunia's men were no good as spies, Razia managed to have a few messages brought from Delhi by some of her trusted slaves. From them she learnt how her marriage had upset the new Sultan, Behram, and how the Amirs were nervous about their future. Only her relative Balban kept calm and showed astuteness and courage in the face of the new development. He prepared the Sultan to encounter what he considered the greatest threat to Behram's rule. Consequently, an immediate mobilisation of forces was ordered. The Amirs were told to close their ranks and join the Sultan in defeating the combined might of Razia and Altunia. Instead of being on the defensive, waiting for Razia to reach Delhi and then engaging her in battle, it was decided to mount the offensive against the forces of Razia and Altunia and meet them far away from the capital.

There were also other reasons for this move. Razia's popularity in Delhi was well known; once she reached the capital the people would rise in support of her. As a commander, Altunia was unrivalled; he had a reputa-

tion alike for the speed and the fury of his strokes; the
only way to humble him was to overwhelm him at the
very first encounter. Balban explained to the Sultan the
various strategies, and persuaded him to lead the imperial
forces in person. The organisation, in every sense, was
complete; the preparations, thorough; and their determination to win, resolute. For this was a challenge to
the very existence of the Forty Amirs. They knew that
if Razia and Altunia won, there was no hope for either
the new Sultan, for Balban and the rest of them or even
for the new order, which their oligarchic clique had so
cleverly and successfully worked to bring about. In
short, all that they had gained would be lost for ever!

Equally anxious were Razia and Altunia to crush the
usurpers in Delhi and regain the throne. The forces at
their disposal were not small; most of Altunia's army was
well knit, being composed of regulars and manned by
first-rate officers. After her defeat at Bhatinda, Razia's
army had, no doubt, disintegrated and become scattered;
but it could be reorganised and put in fit condition.
Then there were the forces of the two powerful Amirs,
Malik Qaraqash and Malik Salari, who were equally
dissatisfied with the state of affairs of the Sultanate and
had offered their co-operation to Razia and Altunia.
The team was powerful enough to challenge the set-up
in Delhi; it decided, therefore, without any loss of time,
to march with their combined forces to the capital.

Another factor, which encouraged them in this undertaking, was the magnificent response of the Hindu population—in particular of the Khokars, Jats and Rajputs.
They responded enthusiastically to the call of Razia, for
to them she was the embodiment of justice, kindness and
fairplay. They remembered with feelings of gratitude her
single-minded struggle against the Forty Amirs to give
the Hindus a better place under the sun; her abolition

of the *Jazziah*; her spirit of accommodation and desire for co-existence with the Hindu rajas; her heroic efforts to lessen their economic burden; her anxiety to redress their grievances; and, above all, her faith in the inter-dependence of the ruler and the ruled. Hence in her hour of need, her Hindu subjects rallied round her in their thousands and took up arms to uphold her inalienable right to the throne of Delhi.

Razia was, indeed, the first Muslim ruler who tried to integrate the indigenous Hindu population with the ruling Muslim class; the first to realise that there could be no lasting peace and security in the Kingdom unless the Hindus were associated with the affairs of the Sultanate and the Hindu rajas were honoured and respected; the first to impress upon her Amirs that the good will of the subjects was the best protection for a sovereign; and, finally, the first to spread love and understanding among different sections of the people in order to bring them closer together. It is thousand pities that she could remain on the throne for only about three and half-years!

Such a Queen was bound to inspire faith and hope among her followers and when she, along with her valiant husband, Altunia, marched to Delhi, it looked as if destiny marched with them; but, alas, it was to prove otherwise! As soon as their forces came half way to Delhi, the imperial armies attacked them. A fierce battle ensued; both sides fought bravely. But ultimately the imperial forces overwhelmed those of Razia and Altunia, surrounding them first by two movements, one from the north and the other by the south, and then encircling them with the aid of the third force led by the Sultan himself. In number and equipment, the imperial forces were far greater; in training and organisation, much superior. As against a haughty spirit of defiance, there was on the other side cool calculation. With Razia and

Altunia there was not even a small reserve force. Moreover, their artillery was heavily outclassed; it could not give sufficient support to the ground forces to thwart the many-sided thrust of the imperial forces. In a matter of days, the Queen and her gallant husband found themselves outflanked, outmanœuvred and completely beaten.

Razia was asked to surrender, but she refused. What was there for her to live for? Everything she stood for had crumbled before her very eyes. From a distance she saw Altunia engaged in a desperate situation. He was also asked to surrender and was promised pardon. For a moment he hesitate'd—but one look at Razia, and a new defiance possessed him. He fought back and was killed. As his wife, Razia felt elevated. By the manner of his dying he had washed away his sins. It was a moment of glory. She bowed her head in gratitude to God. The few men at her side soon lost their lives one after another, but still the Queen fought on, hopelessly but with renewed defiance. Finally an arrow struck her in the heart and she collapsed and died instantly. The date: October 13, 1240.

Thus ended the career of a remarkable Queen who combined in herself some of the rarest qualities of leadership. Instead of asking why she did not do this or did not do that, one may as well wonder how she was able to do so much in so short a time. There have been historians, including Farishta, who have assailed her virtue; but it has now been established on the authority of Isami and others that, even in her relationship with Yaqut, she was above reproach.

The truth is that in many ways Razia was far in advance of her age. She had a breadth of vision which none of her Amirs possessed; a catholicity of outlook which was alien to the demands of the time; a liberalism which seemed strange in those dark days; and, above all, an unshakable belief in justice and fair play which she practised fearlessly. She treated her subjects as a mother would treat her children.

Ruling in a foreign land, and surrounded by bigotry and fanaticism, she struggled to make the subjugated Hindus a part of her Kingdom. May be, she tried to do too many things in too short a time; may be she was too radical for her times; but she shone as a beacon-light in the violence, abandon and grandeur of her era. By the sheer force of her own momentum she generated a new force in India which sought to give a liberal and humane touch to the foundations of Muslim rule. From the beginning she faced storms; by courage and imagination she turned some of them into showers of hope and assurance for the future, but the narrowness and sectarianism of the times overpowered her. And in consequence before the seeds she sowed could grow and fructify, the fields became parched. In the prime of her youth, Razia left the Indian scene. Had she lived and ruled a little longer, she would, instead of the great Moghul, Akbar, have ranked in the annals of India as the pioneer of the movement of national integration!

The mainsprings of her life were courage and conviction, intelligence and common sense, a passion for excellence and a longing for perfection—above all, a burning pride in her father's Kingdom and a deep love of her subjects, irrespective of race and creed. These acted to inspire in her an unremitting confidence in the future, which eluded her every time she tried to grasp it. But nothing daunted her; she faced every crisis bravely and met every challenge resolutely. When she died, she was not even thirty years of age, and with her died a woman of fascinating intellect, vibrant energy and mighty determination, who—in a man's world—brought some relief from man's inhumanity to man, upheld the principles of decency in public life and raised higher the torch of civilisation in the mediæval age.

Weep not for her! Her memory is the shrine
Of pleasant thoughts, soft as the scent of flowers,
Calm as on windless eve the sun's decline,
Sweet as the song of birds among the bowers,
Rich as rain with its hues of light
Pure as the moonshine of an autumn night,
Weep not for her!

PART TWO

THE EPILOGUE

The essentials of historical science are the examination and verification of facts, the careful investigation of the causes, which brought about those facts, and a sound knowledge of the manner, in which events have taken place or have been born.

—IBN KHALDUN
the doyen of Arab historians

I

TRUTH, it is said, is sometimes stranger than fiction; so is the story of Razia. In the short span of her life and in the much shorter period of her rule there was so much of drama that many readers, on reading my account of this Queen, are inclined to treat it more as fiction than as history. That, I am afraid, would be unfair both to Razia and her biographer. Apart from being the only reigning Queen, who ever sat on the throne of Delhi, she was in many ways a remarkable woman. Comparisons are odious but Razia has certainly as much claim on a historian as Cleopatra, whose life has been so artistically dramatised by so many writers, historians and others. On the other hand, Razia's life possessed all the drama, but owing to slim and scanty material, she and her achievements have remained neglected.

For more than seven years now I have been working on the theme of Razia's life; it fascinated me, though the recorded material was hardly sufficient for a biography of the Queen. But even from the short accounts, appearing in such well-known works as the *Cambridge History of India* or the Bharatiya Vidya Bhavan's monumental *History and Culture of the Indian People*, there was enough to attract a discerning eye and to inspire genuine research for truth in order to give Razia's existence a greater reality.

II

My task was, by no means, easy. One of the most original—and perhaps the most reliable—sources regarding this period is the work *Tabakat-i-Nasiri*, written by the chronicler of the times, Minhajus Seraj. But it is no history in our sense of the term; it is neither exhaustive nor scientifically objective. Further, the last twenty years of Minhaj's life were spent in the service of Balban, who was the chief instrument of the destruction of Razia's rule. Minhaj not only outlived Razia by more than two decades but continued in the employment of her traducers, receiving high offices and honours at their hands, with the result that he emphasised in his treatment of Razia such facts as suited his purpose, omitted those which might have embarrassed his subsequent patrons, and invented some in order to help his narration. And still, Minhaj remains our most reliable authority on the events of the times; that is why every other history, mediæval or modern, dealing with this period, is based on his chronicle. Subsequent historians have hailed his *Tabakat-i-Nasiri* as a great work. Farishta is full of praise about it; it has been called a " precious work " by Anquietil du Perron. Elphinstone regarded it as a work of highest consequence; while Stewart relied upon it as " a very valuable book ". I have also broadly adopted the outline of Razia's career as given by Minhaj in his *Tabakat-i-Nasiri*; but my treatment of the material is different from others who have written about her. By and large, they rely on Minhaj not only in regard to facts but even in their interpretation. I have, on the other hand, followed a somewhat different course; I have taken the facts from Minhaj, added to or modified them from other sources, coloured them in the light of my understanding of the events, and then recast them to suit the atmosphere of the times.

III

In this endeavour, I have followed the three methods as outlined by Prof. Arnold Toynbee:

The first is the ascertainment and recording of ' facts '; the second is the elucidation, through a comparative study of the facts ascertained, of ' general laws '; the third is the artistic recreation of the facts in the form of ' fiction '.

Some purists may not be happy about this approach; but as Prof. Toynbee explains at length:

History, like the drama and the novel, grew out of mythology, a primitive form of apprehension and expression in which, as in fairy tales listened to by children or in dreams dreamt of by sophisticated adults, the line between fact and fiction is left undrawn. It has, for example, been said of the *Iliad* that anyone who starts reading it as history will find that it is full of fiction but, equally, anyone who starts reading it as fiction will find that it is full of history. All histories resemble the *Iliad* to this extent, that they cannot entirely dispense with the fictional element. The mere selection, arrangement and presentation of facts is a technique belonging to the field of fiction, and popular opinion is right in its insistence that no historian can be ' great ' if he is not also a great artist; that the Gibbons and Macaulays are greater historians than the ' Dryasdusts ' (a name coined by Sir Walter Scott—himself a greater historian in some of his novels than in any of his ' histories ') who have avoided their more inspired confreres' factual inaccuracies.

There are historians, and very eminent ones, at that, who insist, " let the facts speak for themselves ". But facts are not necessarily capable of speaking for themselves. Much more so in history than in any other area of human life. As Prof. Carl L. Becker puts it:

> Well, for twenty years I have taken it for granted that no one could longer believe so preposterous an idea. But the notion continues to bob up regularly; and only the other day, riding on the train to the meeting of the Historical Association, Mr. A. J. Beveridge, the eminent and honoured historian, assured me dogmatically (it would be dogmatically) that the historian has nothing to do but ' present all the facts and let them speak for themselves.' And so I repeat, what I have been teaching for twenty years, that this notion is preposterous; first because it is impossible to present all the facts; and second, because even if you could present all the facts, the miserable things wouldn't say anything, would say just nothing at all.

IV

However, before I come to Razia and her rule and to my treatment of her personality, her character and her leadership of the Sultanate, I may be forgiven if I digress a bit and describe, at the outset, both the personality of the author Minhaj and the nature of his work. This is necessary in order to judge the man and his observations. As the great Belgian historian, Henri Pirenne writes:

> And this judgment depends necessarily upon the training, the intelligence, and the honour of the witness, as well as upon the circumstances which surrounded the gathering of this evidence. Not only is it indispensable to understand

thoroughly what he wanted to say but to extract from his words whatever of truth lies in them.

Tabakat-i-Nasiri is a general and not specialised history; it begins with the earliest times and ends at about the year 1259, that is about twenty years after the death of Razia. The author's full name was Abu Umar Minhajuddin Usmanibu Sirajuddin Al-Juziani. In an autobiographical account, Minhaj traces his ancestor in the third degree to one Imam Abdul Khalik, who came to Ghazni from Juzjan, the place between Merv and Balkh in Central Asia, in search of a wife. Being an enterprising man, he soon won the confidence of the ruler, Ibrahim, who gave one of his forty daughters, in marriage to him. From this marriage, Abdul Khalik had a son, whom he named Ibrahim. Ibrahim had a son Usman; Usman had a son, Sirajuddin; and it was this Sirajuddin, who was the father of Minhaj.

Minhaj grew up as a man of distinction and acquired favours in the Court of the Ghoris at Delhi; he was given such titles by the reigning monarch as *Ajubatuz Zaman* or "the Wonder of the Time" or *Afshaul Ajam* or the "Orator from Persia". Around 1227, he came to India and was put in charge of the Firozi College of Uch by Nasiruddin Kubacha, the Governor of the territory, who had revolted against Sultan Iltutmish and declared his independence. The Sultan marched against Kubacha, defeated him and then killed him. Minhaj sought an audience with Iltutmish and impressed him sufficiently as to be brought by the Sultan along with him in his train to Delhi. The next year Iltutmish took him on his seige of Gwalior, where the Sultan appointed him, first as a court preacher and then as the "law officer and director of preaching and of all religious, moral and judicial affairs". He continued in that position, until 1238, when Razia as the Queen of the Sultanate, ordered the abandoning of the fort of Gwalior, and the return of all her officers. On his arrival at Delhi, Minhaj was appointed Principal of the Nasiri College, which her illustrious father had founded. On the death of the Queen, Minhaj continued in the service of the Sultan Behram, who made him the Chief Kazi of the Sultanate. Then came the reign of Sultan Nasiruddin Mahmud and the strong man of the realm, Giasuddin Balban; Minhaj served them so ably and loyally that he received favour after favour from them until they honoured him with the title of *Sadr-i-Jahan* or ' the Choice of the World '. In deep gratitude to the Sultan, Minhaj named his monumental work: *Tabakat-i-Nasiri*; it breaks off rather abruptly in the fifteenth year of the reign of Sultan Nasiruddin Mahmud, who remained on the throne of Delhi for twenty years. Minhaj survived Sultan Mahmud and died probably in the early years of the rule of his successor, Balban, about whom he writes in the most eulogistic terms.

V

The other original sources of this period are the manuscripts of Fakhr-i-Mudabbir called *Adab-ul Harb* in the British Museum and *Adab-ul-Muluk* in the India Office Library and his monumental work *Bahrul Ansab*, a portion of which has been edited by the famous orientalist, Sir Denison Ross. Then there is Sadruddin Hasan Nizami's *Tajul Ma'asir*. But neither of the two authors has achieved the eminence of Minhaj, nor have their works acquired the reliability or acceptability of *Tabakat-i-Nasiri*. Hasan Nizami was more a man of letters than a historian; his writings are full of rhetoric, metaphors and euphemism; his style is pedantic and stilted. For years Nizami remained neglected in India and his talents were unrecognised. But in response to a royal announcement inviting scholars to write the history of the conquests of Shahabuddin Ghori he took to historical writing. But it was done more with an eye to please the rulers than to present an objective picture. True, he took much pains over his work, but since he lacked the historian's touch, it falls short of historical requirements.

Fakhr-i-Mudabbir came from a family which had close associations with the Gaznavides. He compiled his *Bahrul Ansab* at Lahore and dedicated it to Iltutmish. His *Adabul Harb* abounds in descriptions of military conquests, but is singularly silent about the exploits of the Slave Dynasty. Of the later historians, two deserve special mention: Isami and Barani. Isami's grandfather occupied the office of Sipahi Salar in Balban's Army, flourished under the patronage of the various Sultans at Delhi, and died when he was ninety during the reign of Muhammad Tughlak. Isami's account of the early Turkish Sultans entitled *Futuhus Salatin* is, therefore, based on the accounts that were handed down to him by his ancestors.

Similarly, Ziauddin Barani also hailed from a family with long and close associations with the Sultans of Delhi. Barani himself was in employment of Muhammad Tughlak. Though in his *Fatwa-i-Jahandari* Barani does not refer to his sources of information, it is evident that he attempted to scrutinise the facts. Isami, on the other hand, relies mainly on the accounts of the various Sultans as given to him by his grandfather, father and other close associates. His work is full of his own prejudices and is far from objective. But as an artist of the period, he remains unsurpassed; his studies of some of the leading figures of the Sultanate are regarded as masterpieces of literary art. In particular, his portrait of Balban, which he has so graphically painted, is highly commended by some of the modern historians.

The other sources are Yahya Sirhindi's *Tarikh-i-Mubarakshahi* and Ghulam Husain Salim's *Riyazus Salatin*. These also throw much light on this period. But to none of them was the reign of Razia, being so short in terms of time, of much significance. Nor were they concerned with the values for which she stood and which we treasure so much these days; they hardly mattered then and did not possess for them even an academic interest. One fact, however, stands out from all this material, brief and scanty though it is, namely, that Razia was a woman of outstanding qualities. Minhaj describes her as " a great sovereign, sagacious, just, beneficent, the patron of the learned, a dispenser of justice, the cherisher of her subjects and of warlike talent, and was endowed with all the admirable attributes and qualifications necessary for kings." But withal, she was a woman. As Minhaj puts it, " She was endowed with all the qualities befitting a king, but she was not born of the right sex and so in the estimation of men all these virtues were worthless. (May God have mercy on her.)" Razia tried to fight this prejudice and, as Minhaj points out, " donned the tunic and assumed the headdress of a man " and conducted the affairs of her Sultanate as a " King ". Even so, the proud Turkish Maliks and Amirs could not reconcile themselves to her rule, and they continued to plot against her until they succeeded.

VI

But perhaps a more important prejudice that she had to contend with was her attitude of racial tolerance; it manifested itself in two ways. One, her behaviour towards the Abyssinian slave, Jamaluddin Yaqut; and two, her concern for her subjects which made Minhaj describe her as "the cherisher of her subjects". Razia's fondness for Yaqut is an accepted fact; how far that fondness went is a matter of interpretation. All that Minhaj says, in this respect, is that Yaqut "acquired favour or closeness in attendance upon the Queen with the result that the Turkish Amirs and Maliks became jealous of him." There is a verse, attributed to Minhaj, which some historians have pounced upon to establish a sinful relationship between Razia and Yaqut; it reads:

عنان تافت دولت ز پیرا منش

چو گردی سیه دید بر دامنش

Good Fortune turned its back on her
No sooner it saw black dust on her skirt.

However, Major H. G. Raverty, in a critical note on his translation of *Tabakat-i-Nasiri*, has tried to prove that the original manuscript did not contain the above lines, and asserted that these must be an inspired interpolation by someone who had reasons to do so. Nor do these lines fit into the context in which they have been interpolated. Nevertheless, the damage to the character of the Queen was done, for many historians who followed Minhaj have enlarged upon these lines and cast all sorts of aspersions upon Razia. Farishta led the attack and has been the most damaging. To quote his words,

> The wise and discerning persons know wherefrom rose this storm of destruction and uprooted the tree of Razia's fortune; indeed, what pretence has an Abyssinian slave to the office of the Amirul Umra at Delhi and what can such depraved rascals have to do with the leadership of the Sultanate of such a Queen?

Budaoni was equally harsh; he is regarded as the authority for having imputed "unchastity" to Razia; but the Persian word he uses is *satar* which Lt.-Col. G. S. A. Ranking in his *Translation of Budaoni's Work* renders as "chastity", while it should really be translated as "seclusion". But both these historians, whose very style of writing makes it clear that they were far from objective in their assessment of Razia, rely on *Tabakat-i-Akbari,* which states that "Yaqut put his hand under Razia's arms and placed her on the animal she rode ". Even if this were a fact, to draw from it the conclusion that there was something sinful in the relationship between the two or to condemn Yaqut, on this account, as a rascal, was stretching it too far; such an adverse deduction cannot stand the test of historical objectivity. True, the observation of the great Arab traveller, Ibn Batuta, who preceded Farishta, is also unfavourable; he records, what must have been obviously told to him by some imaginative persons relishing the talk of such relationship, that Razia "was imputed of having connection with one of her Abyssinian slaves ". In olden times such connection necessarily meant something wrong, especially between an unmarried male and an unmarried female; but a deeper scrutiny of Razia's character and the esteem in which Yaqut held her demolishes any such imputation. That is why Isami, despite his dislike of Razia, refuses in his work *Futuhus Salatin,* to be a party to any such imputation as it was not warranted by facts; even the following verses by him emphasise more the danger to the throne due to the growing power of Yaqut rather than any disgraceful conduct on the latter's part or any reflection on the character of the Queen:

کزین گونہ کین دیو در ملک جم

مسخر تو آمد ز جملہ خدم

عجب نے کہ گر دست یا بد کہے

بے نص خاتم بگیرد رہے

Of all the servants of State
He is the one who has vanquished
So many demons in the Kingdom
That who can really be surprised
If now he tries his hand even at the signet ring.

Relying on the text of Minhaj, Yahya Sarhindi, in his *Tarikh-i-Mubarakshahi,* talks of the *qurbat* or closeness of Yaqut with the Queen; and so does Haji Dabir, who writes that " Yaqut continued getting promotions to the higher ranks until the

Turkish Maliks became jealous of him and felt ashamed of themselves ". There are many others who have underlined this fact of jealousy among the Amirs and held it as one of the major factors in the overthrow of Razia's rule. It would be historically incorrect to deny the closeness between Razia and Yaqut; but there is not a shred of evidence, beyond this simple fact, to show that their relationship was illicit or that Razia, with all the strict religious training that she had, could have erred. Moreover, Altunia would never have married her if he was not convinced of her chastity—an attribute which was held in the highest regards in those days, when marriage with an unchaste woman, however highly placed, would have incurred the wrath of the public and deprived such an alliance of any sanctity or respect in the eyes of the people. And still a reliable nineteenth century historian like Edward Thomas has fallen a prey to the insinuation of unreliable reporters and assailed Razia's character in the following words:

It was not that a virgin Queen was forbidden to love—she might have indulged in a submissive Prince consort, or revelled almost unchecked in the dark recesses of the Palace Harem, but wayward fancy pointed in a wrong direction and led her to prefer a person employed about her Court, an Abyssinian moreover, the favours extended to whom the Turki nobles resented with one accord.

A good historian should avoid moral condemnation especially where evidence is so slim and sketchy; in this case, there are so many factors which lead us overwhelmingly to a different conclusion. Even Minhaj has nothing but the highest praise for the upbringing and character of Razia; no one, with any modicum of historical understanding, therefore, would agree with the denunciation of the Queen and Yaqut indulged in by Farishta and others.

As Prof. Herbert Butterfield observes in *History and Human Relations*:

. . . the moral judgments of historians are so often taken at a low level; we might even say that these things are almost invariably more rough-and-ready than anything else in the whole complicated fabric of historical writing. In reality they are pseudo-moral judgments, masquerading as moral ones,

mixed and muddy affairs, part prejudice, part political ani-
mosity with a dash of ethical flavouring wildly tossed into the
concoction.

Elaborating his contention, he points out:

It has even happened that the devout and reasonably
virtuous person, who at certain periods would have needed
exceptional saintliness or real originality of mind to break
away from the prevalent principles of persecution, has suffered
greatly at the hand of such historians, while the irreligious
scoundrel, pursuing toleration from worldly-mindedness and
motives of real politic, has been able to emerge with un-
deserved honours. Moral judgments are the more apt for
this reason to be political ones in disguise—the historian is
seeking to add a sort of supercharge to his condemnation of
a certain policy.

Prof. Butterfield takes the case of the massacre of St. Bartho-
lomew and explains:

Let us say that we have assembled around Catherine de
Medici everything that may have reference to the affair—all
that we can discover of her predicament at the time, of preceding events, of her own constitution and structure, of her
views, her intentions and motives, as well as all that we can
discover of the range of options which was open to her at
the decisive moment. Assisted by all this material and by
all the humanity we possess, we are now called on to resurrect
the whole occasion and to see with Catherine, feel with her,
hold our breath with her, and meet the future with all her
apprehensions. If by imaginative sympathy we can put ourselves in her place in this way, not only envisaging the situation in all its detail but apprehending it in all its vividness
and intensity until we reach the point at which we could
almost conceive ourselves making the drastic decision, or at
least have a sense of just what it would take to carry us across
the border to such a decision—then we are historians indeed.

VII

In regard to Razia's marriage with Altunia, as is universally
accepted, it was not only approved by their followers but it

became the focal point of a massive revolt against the usurpers of the Queen's throne at Delhi; it is in the light of this development, and the logic behind it, that I have attempted to resurrect the whole occasion, to discover Razia's predicament at the time, and to make the readers feel with her and meet the future with all her apprehensions.

From the scarce material available about her rule, it is also clear that Razia believed, right from the beginning, in the welfare of her subjects and took many steps to safeguard their interest; she moved among them freely and listened to their grievances personally. They idolised her but this upset the Amirs and Maliks and ranged them still more firmly against the Queen. These have been explained at appropriate places in my study of Razia, and further elaboration would serve no useful purpose. Minhaj has, no doubt, a word of praise, here and there, but, on the whole, his attitude was no less unsympathetic to the Queen than that of the Amirs and Maliks. That is why he describes the end of Razia in a most ridiculous manner; after the final battle, where the contending forces mustered all their strength, Minhaj makes Razia hide in some corner, where some Hindu robbers are said to have killed her. No more fantastic statement could have been made; it cannot stand the test of history for a moment. Does such a behaviour fit into the personality of the Queen, whom Minhaj himself describes as possessing " fighting talents "? Is it possible for the leader of a movement, which was ruthlessly crushed, to run away from the battlefield and seek shelter behind a tree? If robbers killed her, what was the proof that they were Hindus? The whole version is a figment of Minhaj's imagination; he tried to underplay the significance of this struggle and the martyrdom of Razia; he was careful enough not to disgrace the name of his chief patron, Balban, or to make Nasiruddin Mahmud, after whom he named his *Tabakat-i-Nasiri*, appear as a usurpur; moreover, according to Isami, Razia fought along with Altunia not one but two battles before she was finally vanquished—a version which again contradicts the account given by Minhaj. Minhaj was also proud of his Islamic background and knowledge; he knew the Quran by heart and was well versed in the Traditions. As the Chief Kazi of the Sultanate in the reign of Nasiruddin Mahmud, he was often consulted by the Sultan and his opinions were respected. But withal, he remained a Turk, proud of his tribal lineage; even towards the Indian Muslims, leave aside the Hindus, his attitude was far from sympathetic. This is evident from the manner in which he has written about Imamuddin Rayhan and from his lack of sympathy for and understanding of the problems of the Hindu rajas. That is why his chronicle is full of the glories of the various Sultans; but it throws little light on the condition of their subjects. True, unlike the histories written by the Arab historians, which deal with all aspects of a rule, the Persian historians concentrated mainly on the rulers and their activities, with hardly any mention about the economic or social condition of the people. They had no *usul-isnad* or the rule of investigating a narrative, like the Arab historical writers, who traced a narrative to a reliable eye-witness before accepting and recording it; *Hadith* or the science of the Traditions of the Prophet was developed on the basis of this rule. The approach of a Persian historian, on the other hand, was much less scientific. He concerned himself with the court and the palace, and wrote with an eye on royal pleasure. Minhaj not only cared for his Sultan but took care to see, in all his observations, that he was on the right side of the Turkish oligarchy.

His other two contemporaries were less servile; but all three were motivated by a genuine desire to justify the deeds and actions of the Muslim rulers. Of them Hasan Nizami's account is hardly historical; Fakhr-i-Mudabbir is more theological; only Minhaj writes as a historian, is reasonably careful to marshal his facts, and has given in his *Tabakat-i-Nasiri* chronological data, which are, by and large, reliable.

VIII

I must, however, admit that in reconstructing the different aspects and phases of Razia's life I have taken liberties, here and there, which may not be approved by the purists. I may even be charged with arbitrariness; my approach may be considered more in line with that of a historical novelist than that of a historian. And still, with the scanty material available to me, there was no alternative if I were ever to succeed in recapturing the atmosphere of the times and in bringing Razia to life. After all, as Macaulay said, history is simply a " branch of

literature ", and the job of a " truly great historian " is to
" reclaim the materials which the novelist has appropriated ".
Undoubtedly, he cannot do so with the same ease and freedom
as a novelist can; a historian in giving vent to his imagination
must subject himself, unlike the artist, to the discipline of factual evidence and criticism. In describing the end of Razia,
for instance, I have not deviated from the main factual evidence
as recorded by Minhaj. But I have interpolated something,
here and there, which I feel fits in more with the accepted pattern of Razia's personality. In doing so I have relied on the
advice as offered by the greatest English philosopher-historian
of our time, Mr. Bradley, in his well-known treatise on *The
Presuppositions of Critical History.* In it he asked the question:
could the historian, after a critical scrutiny of his authorities,
say that though authorities record this, what really happened
must have been not this but that? Replying in the affirmative
he explained that if the historian's experience of worldly affairs
obliged him to disbelieve what the authorities recorded, then
he must abide by his own judgment. Even Prof. R. G. Collingwood, though critical of Bradley, admits that, in addition to
selecting from among his authorities' statements those which he
regards as important, the historian must in two ways go beyond
what his authorities tell him. One is the critical way and the
other is the constructive way. In both, imagination plays a
role, though in one case it may be more arbitrary or fanciful
and in the other more restricted and careful. As a result, the
historian's picture of the past in many details may be more
imaginative and even imaginary. He may develop a resemblance to a novelist. There is, however, no need to be apologetic about it; as Prof. Collingwood observes:

> Each of them makes it his business to construct a picture
> which is partly a narrative of events, partly a description of
> situations, exhibition of motives, analysis of characters. Each
> aims at making his picture a coherent whole, where every
> character and every situation is so bound up with the rest
> that this character in this situation cannot but act in this way,
> and we cannot imagine him as acting otherwise. The novel
> and the history must both of them make sense; nothing is
> admissible in either except what is necessary, and the judge
> of this necessity is in both cases the imagination. Both the

novel and the history are self-explanatory, self-justifying, the product of an autonomous or self-authorizing activity; and in both cases this activity is the *a priori* imagination. As works of imagination, the historian's work and the novelist's do not differ. Where they do differ is that the historian's picture is meant to be true. The novelist has a single task only: to construct a coherent picture, one that makes sense. The historian has a double task: he has both to do this, and to construct a picture of things as they really were and of events as they really happened.

In the case of Razia, apart from the three contemporary chronicles, there is no other evidence which could give us any worthwhile factual data about this period of mediæval India; that is why a reconstruction of that evidence is almost inevitable. Further, the chronicles themselves suffer from so many limitations that they are not of as great a help to us as similar documents can be, though how far any such documents are really helpful in the writing of an objective history is a moot point. As the eminent historian, M. Henri Pirenne, writes:

Of all the sources of history, they are at once the most valuable and the most fallacious. The very way in which they have come down to us has almost always changed them more or less seriously. When we have the rare good fortune to possess the original text, its state of preservation generally makes its deciphering more or less difficult—torn or disfigured as it usually is by words left out, smudges, or words written over others. But in most cases the original has disappeared. To reconstitute that text, we have at our disposal mere copies, and often only copies of copies, all in some measure spoiled by negligence, ignorance, or the untrustworthiness of the copyist. But let us assume that this task is accomplished; other problems present themselves. It is important to know the origin of the document, to establish the exact date, to determine its degree of authenticity. Mistakes abound in all epochs, and individuals or governments have invented or modified texts to suit their interests.

Judged by this touchstone even our greatest source *Tabakat-i-Nasiri* cannot be considered absolutely reliable; the wind and the rain have effaced some of its parts; and interpolations and deductions have vitiated the original texts. Further, in considering such texts, one has to be equally careful about its credibility; in fact, this is an indefinitely more delicate and subjective operation. As Pirenne observes:

In spite of all his efforts, therefore, the historian cannot gain an adequate knowledge of what has been. Realizing this limitation, he resigns himself to it. He accepts the limits which the very conditions of the knowledge of real history impose upon written history. To perceive the facts in the measure in which this is possible must suffice. Although in relation to the absolute this is not much, it is still a great deal from the view-point of man.

According to Pirenne, " all historical narrative " is a hypothesis, for, as he remarks:

It is an attempt at explanation, a conjectural reconstitution of the past. Each author throws light on some part, brings certain features into relief, considers certain aspects. The more these accounts multiply, the more the infinite reality is freed from its veils. All these accounts are incomplete, all imperfect, but all contribute to the advancement of knowledge. Those whose results have passed out of date have served to elaborate others which are in their turn replaced.

IX

In writing about Razia, I have been guided by all these considerations; they have helped me in understanding the events and reconstructing the situation; they have emboldened me to describe the rule of Razia, not as an engineer might describe a machine, but as an artist would paint a portrait. In my enthusiasm, it is possible I have been influenced by my biases, prejudices, beliefs and affections; in making the selection and arrangement of facts I may have become involved in a combined and complex intellectual operation, where objectivity might have been sacrificed. To these charges, I must plead guilty. I also agree that a good historian should be free from personal prejudices; Thucydides's dislike of Cleon, for instance, left him to give an inaccurate account of the political history of his times; similarly in recent times, H. G. Wells' *Outline of History* suffers from objectivity because of his antipathy to all military figures; but such prejudice cannot be considered as a serious obstacle to the attainment of truth in history. As the German historian Hans Meyerhoff puts it:

> In short, history cannot be cast into a rational system; nor are its methods entirely rational. Reason is often a poor guide to the deeply hidden, irrational strata from which many of the richest manifestations of human life draw their meaning and sustenance.

One of the earliest historians, Thucydides, who ranks as second in importance to Herodotus, wrote with great artistry. His regard for accuracy did not prevent him, while writing about the conflict of Athens and Sparta in the Peloponnesian war, from giving a presentation which was full of such epic grandeur that it could not but move the Greek mind. Though Thucydides is careful about his facts, he handles his theme so deftly that he brings out in all their poignancy the repeated follies of men, driven as if by destiny, to commit one wrong after another until victory eludes them and they fall irretrievably into ruin and disaster.

Herder, who was the first historian to appeal to the principle of empathy, rightly urged that one must feel oneself into a period, into life, and into history as a whole. Like the artist the historian must recreate a character; develop the sense of the times; be in tune with the spirit of resurgence; and re-enact the past experience in the living thought of the present. Towards this end, he must draw upon imagination and with sympathy and understanding bring back to life, what had remained almost dead and forgotten, as Tolstoy did in *War and Peace*. Though popularly taken as a novel, this great work is a truer picture of Russian life, set against the background of Napoleon's invasion, than any history; in scope and organisation, it defies description. The book has been classified as historical, sociological, psychological, political, epic, even as a philosophy of history. It has angered historians; annoyed military strategists; exasperated the non-Russian readers with the many classes and groups with which it deals; and confused even the critics. And still it remains one of the best literary creations of all times, presenting events, settings and characters, with such artistic organisation and breadth of vision, that there has been no rival to it either in the depth or scope of historical treatment. A historian must—if he is to succeed with his readers— picturise " past shadows of people and movements, conflicts and victories, landscapes and physical hardships, secret passions and social forces, in their specific and unique characteristics instead of enshrining them in dry-as-dust categories of philosophy ".

X

In my own humble way, I have endeavoured to clothe the different figures in the Turkish oligarchy, which dominated the Sultanate during the three and a half years of Razia's rule, in their different hues and attires, and reconstructed situations so as to give more reality to the stresses and strains of those days. For this purpose I have made use of the cultural renaissance that had overtaken the world of Islam, and quoted from the works of the great philosophers, poets and thinkers, who influenced the intellectual scene. The quotations, which I have put into the mouth of different persons in my study, might not have been used by them; but they are representative of the intellectual approach of those times and in keeping with the atmosphere that prevailed in Delhi in the first half of the thirteenth century. For, this was an age which was dominated by Ghazali and Rumi, Saadi and Khayyam, the Arab philosophers like Ibn Rushd and Ibn Sina, and which saw the birth of many new trends in art and literature, science and humanities. In the exchanges that took place between Razia and her Amirs and Maliks on the role of Islam in subjugated countries, I have made use of the controversies that raged among the different schools of thought and have tried, as best I could, to be authentic about the differing view-points; likewise, the blessings of Allah that Razia seeks on her accession to the throne might not be traced to any contemporary chronicle but they are in the well-known and familiar language of Muslim theology, which has come down to us from the times of the Prophet and the early Caliphs. I cannot, however, deny that my own affiliations and beliefs have probably influenced the emphasis which I have, undoubtedly, given to one trend or the other in describing the life and times of Razia, but can I help it? As Prof. Alan Bullock reveals, a historian " cannot begin to think or explain events without the help of the pre-conceptions, the assumptions, the generalization of experience which he brings with him—and is bound to bring with him—to his work. When Mathiez, for example, began to work on the history of the French Revolution, his mind was not a blank, it was full of views and prejudices about revolutions and their causes, about the way people behave in times of revolution, about the relative importance to be attached to economic and intellectual factors. The historian gives a false account of his activity if he tries to deny the part that general ideas and assumptions play in his work."

In my study of Razia I have been guided by the pre-conceptions, the assumptions and the generalisations of my own experience; these are evident not only in my treatment of Razia but the lesser figures, who played their roles in the drama of her life. Some of them influenced the course of events; some proved to be the obstacles in her way; and some, like Balban, became the cause of her destruction. It is not easy to delineate their characters. I, therefore, drew inspiration in depicting them more from the plays of Shakespeare than the researches of professional historians for, I believe, there is more of English history in the works of the great dramatist than in all the standard text-books that have come out from Oxford and Cambridge. True, Shakespeare was a genius and cannot be emulated; but he can be an ideal for a historian as much as for a playwright.

Take, for instance, the character of Shah Turkan; there is so little of source material about her and still she was such a powerful character that in the hands of a Shakespeare she could have put even Lady Macbeth to shame. Indeed, what a life she lived—starting as a mere concubine, she rose to be the most favourite queen of the great Iltutmish and even after his death, asserted herself in many ways and became a most dominating figure in the whole Sultanate. Her ruthlessness was monumental; her cunning, diabolical. To snatch the throne from Razia in the face of the testamentary declaration by Iltutmish and then to establish a petticoat rule, which, though short-lived, shook the very foundations of the empire, was no mean a task. She did not mind even blinding the ten-year-old child of the late Sultan by another wife and organising a most ingenious plot against Razia so long as these could secure for her a more permanent position at Delhi; her end was pathetic but her career, most colourful and chequered. There are few characters in all history to match her.

I am no dramatist or novelist; but even so I could not treat Shah Turkan in the dry-as-dust manner of a professional historian; to be true to her character I had to try and bring her out in her true colours. In developing her personality I might have re-constructed history but what option did I have if I were to give reality to her existence? Minhaj dismisses her in a few sentences; but books can be written about her. In my endeavour to reason about her actions, I had to go back to her motives and the consequences that followed those motives. But as M. Henri Pirenne rightly asks, "where are these motives and consequences to be found if not in the mind of him who does the reasoning?" The historians are no exception to this; that is why Thucydides is a greater historian than Xenophon and Machiavelli than Froissert. Why, Herodotus—the Father of History—was himself more of a story teller than a historian. His book begins with the story that Candaules, who was sorry that no one except himself knew the beauty of his Queen, wished to be envied. Unknown to the Queen he, therefore, hid his Prime Minister Gyges behind a curtain so that the latter might have a good look at the Queen, while she took bath naked. The Queen, however, saw the feet of the Prime Minister sticking out and took immediate offence. She caught him and warned, "Either you must die for this or kill the King and marry me." Gyges was happy to make the choice; he killed the King and founded his own dynasty. Herodotus is full of many such amusing stories.

XI

To go back to Minhaj, he did not lack the vigour and penetration of mind, which are essential for a historian; but he could not have the variety of knowledge and depth of understanding that a modern chronicler possesses and, therefore, lacked the necessary historical imagination or psychological understanding. To him Razia's friendship with Yaqut was a lapse; he implies it in his work *Tabakat-i-Nasiri* though does not say it in so many words, as we have pointed out earlier. Razia's marriage with Altunia was to him a desirable development for it represented the restoration of a covetous virtue, which he attributed to the fallen Queen. He was unable to understand that she could be in love with both Yaqut and Altunia and still not be guilty of any lapse. Trained in the orthodox way of life, Minhaj could not comprehend a dual involvement of such emotional nature, where, the love of one did not exclude the love for the other.

As the great English poet, Shelley, has put it:

True Love in this differs from gold and clay,
That to divide is not to take away.

To us this may be a reflection of the broad humanism which was the motivating force of Razia's life; but to Minhaj it could not but be a weakness involving moral turpitude. Farishta and others take the clue and elaborate upon the lapse—no doubt beyond all proportions—for to them, it was not only unethical but immoral. As the modern philosopher, Prof. Stebbing, remarks: " Even if ethical principles are eternal and immutable it is certain that they need to be re-interpreted for every period and re-thought for every generation. Our moral beliefs, our standards of right and wrong, our conception of our relations to other men undergo some change as our modes of living change."

Despite these limitations, in respect to both his background and his approach, Minhaj was and remains a great historian; likewise his *Tabakat-i-Nasiri* contains a mine of information. It provides the base for this period, without which no super-structure is possible. True, it suffers from many shortcomings; it is, for instance, completely silent about the social aspect of the period, without which any political history, as G. M. Trevelyan says, " is unintelligible ". There are no reports in it about the human and economic relations of different classes, or of the character of family, or household life, or the conditions of labour and of lesser people, or of the culture of that age, which must have influenced religion, literature, music, architecture and the whole gamut of learning and thought.

Moreover this was the time when Islam began to make some deep impact on Hinduism, especially through the teachings of the Sufis, who, in turn, were influenced by the local Hindu environment; but there is little of this to be found in the works of the contemporary chroniclers. Three hundred years later this "assimilation between the two great civilisations" had been so cemented that Babur described it as "the Hindustani way". In bringing about this "assimilation", Razia played the pioneering role; but neither Minhaj nor the other chroniclers of the times had the eyes to see it or the heart to feel it. What a pity! For, as Sir John Marshall has observed, ". . . seldom in the history of mankind has the spectacle been witnessed of two civilisations, so vast and so strongly developed, yet so radically dissimilar as the Muhammadan and Hindu, meeting and mingling together." Minhaj and his contemporaries wrote in the same manner as did the mediæval historians of Europe, who were mainly concerned about the conflict of Christianity with paganism; in their anxiety to justify their particular view-points they ignored other events. Undoubtedly they have bequeathed to posterity valuable material of that period; but, as historians, they cannot be freed from certain theological and moral lapses; nor can their work be really considered objective for no history is objective. And still it would be wrong on our part to condemn their contribution as a mere matter of taste; it would be like damning mediæval astronomy as bogus in the light of modern science.

What we should guard against is that emotional prejudices should not bedevil a historian's judgment; in other respects his freedom must remain unfettered. He cannot be expected to be a mere collector of facts; nor are there in reality such things as "facts duly assembled in a library or a laboratory", which could automatically and inexorably suggest or dictate their own conclusions in all cases"; some facts are known, some are not; and of even those, which are known, only a few can be selected and then arranged so as to make history. That is why our approach to historical writing must change as we acquire more variety of knowledge and experience; in fact, with the passage of time, our understanding of what really happened in the past improves for new issues are thrown up and these help us to re-write the story of the past. As the great American philosopher John Dewey puts it,

Intelligent understanding of past history is to some extent a lever for moving the present into a certain kind of future. No historic present is a mere redistribution, by means of permutations and combinations, of the elements of the past.

Men are engaged neither in a mechanical transposition of the conditions they have inherited, nor yet in simply preparing for something to come after. They have their own problems to solve; their own adaptations to make. They face the future, but for the sake of the present, not of the future. In using what has come to them as an inheritance from the past they are compelled to modify it to meet their own needs, and this process creates a new present in which the process continues. History cannot escape its own process.

XII

In presenting the story of Razia I have put together odds and ends found here and there and attempted to make them into one coherent whole. The limitations, as I have already explained, were many; the handicaps, innumerable; the material, slim, scanty and scattered; but at the same time, I had a peculiar feeling for the subject and, therefore, I have used the material in the same manner as a potter uses the clay or the mason, the stone, fashioning it to my heart's desire. I cannot deny the love for the subject which inspired in me the confidence to discard what I did not approve and to find out what I needed for my purpose. I was even helped by my own intuition—that leap of mind, which made explanations easy; situations, coherent and complications, understandable. I do not know to what extent I have succeeded and even if the result of my efforts appears to be fragmentary or at times even faulty, I have no regrets, for throughout I was guided by my own idea of what ought to be. Authorities did not frighten me; chronicles did not unnerve me. They were no doubt extremely useful and I made full use of them; so did I make use of libraries, archives and museums—" the silent white abodes of the dead "—which store for us records and documents; legends and stories; urns, coins, medals and seals; implements and ornaments; charters and manuscripts. I also examined ruins, columns and graves. But all these aids could not bring out the inner spirit of history. Nor were the scholars, engaged in unearthing the past, of any greater help; they were, no doubt, good companions on the road to the fulfilment of my objective but I could not accept them—to use the words of Benedetto Croce as used in his classic, *History—Its Theory and Practice*, as if " they have history under lock and key " and that " they are people, who unlock the ' sources ' by which thirsty humanity may quench its desire for knowledge ". On the contrary, as Croce observes ". . . we know that history is in all of us and that its sources are in our breasts. For it is in our own breasts alone that is to be found that crucible in which the *certain* is converted into the *true* and *philology*, joining with *philosophy*, produces *history* ".

The Razia, that has emerged from the preceding pages, is as real as any historical figure of that era; but she is as much the product of the historical material as of the urge within my own breast.

20 July 1966   RAFIQ ZAKARIA

BIBLIOGRAPHY

(A) ORIGINAL SOURCES

Minhajus Seraj: *Tabakat-i-Nasiri*
English Translation: By H. G. Raverty
Fakhruddin Mubarak Shah (better known as Fakhr-e-Mudabbir):
Baharul Ansab—A Portion edited by Denison Ross
Adab-ul Harb
Sadruddin Hasan Nizami: *Tajul Maasir*
Isami: *Futuh-us Salatin*
Ibn Battuta: *Kitabur Rahlah*
Abridged English Translation by H. A. R. Gibb
Yahya bin Ahmad Sirhindi: *Tarikh-i-Mubarakshahi*
Ziauddin Barani: *Fatawa-i-Jahandari*
English Translation by Prof. Habib and Dr. Afsar Afzaluddin
Ziauddin Barani: *Tarikh-i-Firoz Shahi*
Nizamuddin Ahmad Bakhshi: *Tabaqat-i-Akbari*
Muhammad Qasim Farishta: *Gulshan-i-Ibrahimi*
Abdul Qadir Budauni: *Muntakhab-ut-Tawarikh*
Ghulam Hussain Salim: *Riyazus Salatin*
Abu Raihan and Beruni: *Kitabul Hind*
Haji Dabir: *Zafarle-Walihi*

(B) SECONDARY WORKS

— — — : *The Cambridge Medieval History*, Vol. II
— — — : *The Cambridge History of India*, Vol. III
Bharatiya Vidya Bhavan: *The History and Culture of the Indian People*, Vol. V
V. A. Smith: *The Oxford History of India*
A. B. M. Habibullah: *The Foundation of Muslim Rule in India*
H. M. Elliot and J. Dawson: *History of India as told by its own Historians*, Vol. II
Edward Thomas: *Chronicles of the Pathan Kings of Delhi*
Aziz Ahmad: *Political History and Institutions of the Early Turkish Empire of Delhi*
C. V. Vaidya: *History of Medieval Hindu India*
S. H. Hodivala: *Studies in Indo-Muslim History*
James Todd: *Annals and Antiquities of Rajasthan*
Tara Chand: *Influence of Islam on Indian Culture*
I. H. Qureshi: *Administration of the Sultanate of Delhi*
R. P. Tripathi: *Some Aspects of Muslim Administration*
Yusuf Husain: *Glimpses of Medieval India Culture*

Daniel C. D. Donnett: *Conversion and the Poll Tax in Early Islam*

Syed Ameer Ali: *A Short History of the Saracens*

Syed Ameer Ali: *Spirit of Islam*

Dr. Mohamed Iqbal: *The Reconstruction of Religious Thought in Islam*

Carr Stephen: *Archæology and Monumental Remains of India*

P. Hardy: *Historians of Mediæval India*

F. W. Thomas: *Mutual Influence of Muhammedans and Hindus in India*

Khaliq Ahmad Nizami: *Some Aspects of Religion & Politics in India during the 13th Century*

T. W. Arnold: *Preaching of Islam*

Sir Syed Ahmad Khan: *Asarus Sanadid*

H. Nelson Wright: *Coinage and Metrology of the Sultans of Delhi*

Stanley Lane-Poole: *Mediæval India under Mohammadan Rule*

Ishwari Prasad: *Mediæval India*

(C) BOOKS CONSULTED FOR THE EPILOGUE

Arnold Toynbee: *A Study of History*

Emery Neff: *The Poetry of History*

Fritz Stern (Ed.): *The Varieties of History*

Geoffrey Barraclough: *History in a Changing World*

H. Butterfield: *History and Human Relations*

F. M. Powicke: *Modern Historians and the Study of History*

Benedetto Croce—Translated by Douglas Ainslee: *History: Its Theory and Practice*

Ibn Khaldun—English Translation by Franz Rosenthal: *Muqaddamah*

R. G. Collingwood: *The Idea of History*

Stuart A. Rice (Ed.): *Methods in Social Sciences*

John Dewey: *Logic: The Theory of Inquiry*

W. H. Walsh: *Introduction to Philosophy of History*

Sir Isaiah Berlin: *Historical Inevitability*

James H. Nichols: *Force and Freedom*

Morris R. Cohen: *The Meaning of History*

Sidney Hook: *From Hegel to Marx*

Sidney Hook: *The Hero in History*

G. J. Renier: *History: Its Purpose and Method*

Jasques Maritian: *On the Philosophy of History*

Reinhold Niebuhr: *Faith and History*

Paul Tillich: *The Interpretation of History*

A. L. Rowse: *The Use of History*

Hans Meyerhoff (selected & edited by): *The Philosophy of History in Our Time: An Anthology*

E. H. Carr: *What is History?*

INDEX

(The names of authors whose works are referred to are given in italics)